LEVEL UP YOUR LIFE

**BUILD MEANINGFUL
HABITS FOR A JOYFUL LIFE**

LISA DRUXMAN

LEVEL UP YOUR LIFE
Copyright ©2024 by Lisa Druxman

All rights reserved. This book or any portion thereof may not be reproduced or used in any manner whatsoever without the express written permission of the publisher except for the use of brief quotations in a book review.

ISBN Ebook: ISBN 979-8-218-50884-5
ISBN Paperback: 979-8-218-50882-1
ISBN Hardcover: 979-8-218-51835-6

THIS BOOK IS DEDICATED TO ALL WHO HELP ME LIVE A LEVEL 10 LIFE.

To Jason, my husband: Thank you for always believing in me, loving me through all my crazy ways, and standing by my side through every adventure.

To my two amazing kids, Jacob and Rachel: My love for you is limitless, beyond a 10. I know you are both destined to live full, extraordinary lives filled with love, joy and happiness.

To my sister: You challenge me to see the things I might overlook, and you inspire me daily with your passion for gardening, fitness, family and life itself.

To my parents: You believed in me even when I didn't believe in myself. Your unconditional love and support have been my foundation, and I am forever blessed to have you in my life.

To my team, past and present: You've not only made an incredible impact on countless moms across the country, but you've also profoundly shaped my journey. For that, I am deeply grateful.

To my wonderful friends: You've brought joy to my life, whether through simple game nights or grand adventures. Thank you for enriching my life with your laughter and love.

And to you, the reader: It is my deepest hope, prayer, and wish that you live your life fully. Don't just exist—be truly alive. May you find your own path to a Level 10 life.

CONTENTS

Introduction	1
1. What Level Is Your Life?	19
2. Grounded in Gratitude	47
3. Going Slowly	57
4. Being Present	65
5. Live with Your Senses	81
6. Your Village	91
7. Purpose	107
8. Fun, Play, Adventure	117
9. Be Addicted to Growing Yourself	127
10. The Gift of Giving	135
11. Get Outside	143
12. Embracing Spirituality	153
Conclusion. The Joy of Living	161

INTRODUCTION

"Life isn't about finding yourself.
Life is about creating yourself."

— **GEORGE BERNARD SHAW**

We are so busy being busy. We are stuck on the hamster wheel. We stare more at screens than into the eyes of our loved ones. We are living life on the surface, rarely going deep. Stress, anxiety, and mental health issues are at an all-time high. We want to be happy, but don't quite know how to get there. We see a giant chasm between where we are and where we want to be.

But in that chasm is your life. The joy is in the journey. The joy is in the simplicity of each day.

It is the experience of living in your real, daily life that needs to be appreciated: the highs and lows, the simplicity of the moment, the appreciation of your breath and body. At the end of your life, you want to look back and know that you found joy in the ride of life. At the end of your life, you want to know that you loved, connected, and had fun more than you scrolled your phone and binged Netflix. You want to know that you lived for the day and not just for weekends or vacations. You want to know that you lived on purpose.

My name is Lisa Druxman. I am the founder and CEO of FIT4MOM, the largest fitness program in the U.S. for moms. We have hundreds of franchisees and thousands of instructors nationwide. I am mom to two awesome, pretty-much-grown-up kids, Jacob and Rachel, and I am wife to Jason.

For the past two decades, women have come to me for answers. As a business owner, podcaster, and writer, thousands have asked me how to balance work and life, prioritize self-care, and escape feeling overwhelmed in their lives. And the truth was, in those early years I hadn't figured it out myself. But I knew I needed to—for them and for myself. I learned how to Level Up my life based on what I learned from my master's degree in psychology, leading a multimillion dollar company, studying ancient wisdom, and a whole lot of personal experimentation. I did figure it out, and that's what I will share with you.

Let me take you back to the beginning. As a kid, I was socially awkward, unsuccessful at school, and totally uncoordinated. I got C's and D's in school. I didn't have any friends. And I was always the last picked for every team at school. I have ADD (yes, diagnosed Attention-Deficit Disorder), and I lived a life of "I can't." "I can't do well in school." "I can't be good in sports." "I can't make friends." I was living below the bar of success in every area of my life. My parents would have bought me the latest in fashion, but I was a bit out of it. My corduroys and vinyl screen-printed baseball shirt with the sparkle horse picture wasn't quite cool. My hair was frizzy and unmanageable. Ladies, these were the days before hair gel and diffusers; I had no idea how to deal with my curly hair. I had no confidence. I tried to do what the other cool girls did. The trend in third grade was creating albums of puffy stickers. Remember the ones with the googly eyes? I was so proud of my page-filled album. Then the "mean girls" stole my stickers and put them on the bottom of their shoes. My heart hurt.

If I were to give my life a score then, it was maybe a four. Realize: I had everything going for me. I had a great family, lived in a nice home, and really wanted for nothing. I have no sob story of pain and poverty to share with you. Some of my dearest and most successful friends tell me about real stories of struggle and hard work. They grew up poor, on farms. They had to milk the goats before school and plow the fields after. I'm serious! I had none of that. I had a beautiful upper-middle-class home and a very supportive family.

I created my own struggle. My mindset and my habits held me back from success in all areas of life. I look back on that little girl and feel sorry for her, because there was no reason to feel like I did.

Then, when I was thirteen, I was held up at gunpoint. Most people say that in these moments, your life flashes before your eyes. But I hadn't had much of a life—I was only thirteen. What passed before me was that I had already lived a life of regret. I regretted that I had not had friends, had not done well in school, had not applied myself at really anything. What could have been a low point in my life became a turning point. I walked away from that incident, and it became my first kick in the pants to Level Up my life.

From that moment on, I started to approach life with new strategies. If you want something different, you need to focus on the different part. I became proactive in my life. I started to put effort into it. When a teacher told me to read a book that felt too overwhelming, I broke it down into chapters. When that chapter was too overwhelming, I broke it down into paragraphs. When that paragraph was too overwhelming, I broke it down into sentences. I did this until I was able to master reading, and then I used this principle of breaking things down into small bites to start hacking my life. I started to apply myself in school, in sports, and with friends. Well, okay, I really didn't apply myself in sports, because I was still too afraid I might hold back a team. So I got into fitness, which was a one-woman sport. I was just responsible for myself.

One of my mentors, Dan Sullivan, talks about the 4 C's: Commitment, Courage, Capability, and Confidence. I first needed to commit that I wanted to create a better life for myself. I then needed to have the courage to try new things and put myself out there. The more I did this, the more I built capability in each area. I got better socially, at school, and in fitness. Capability leads to confidence. The more I did, the more confident I became in what I could achieve in any area of my life.

By the time I went to college, I was fascinated with the mind and how, through mindset and habits, we might be holding ourselves back from living our best lives. To learn more about cognitive and behavioral modification, I pursued my undergraduate degree and my master's degree in psychology. I was a fitness professional in college teaching aerobics (now I just dated myself!) and personal training. I found it fascinating that I would tell my clients to eat grilled chicken and broccoli but then was compelled myself to eat fried chicken and French fries. Who was I kidding? I wondered why I ate the unhealthy choice, even when I knew better. My master's thesis focused on behavior modification weight control. What I learned was that motivation and willpower would wear out, but habits remained. We'll talk more about that later in this book.

On top of my education, I gave myself a chaser of Tony Robbins. Listening to his tapes blew my mind—probably more than my formal education. I became a self-help junkie. I have read self-development books daily for the past three decades. They say that 10,000 hours makes someone an expert. If that's the case, I can now call myself an expert in personal development (365 days x 1 hour per day x 30 years = 10,950 hours). I learned how to change my mindset and my habits and started to build a very successful life through much learning and even more experimentation.

When I became a mom, I started a company called Stroller Strides (now called FIT4MOM). I wasn't looking to start a business. I started it because I wanted and needed community. I knew nothing about motherhood. Stroller Strides is a stroller-based workout where moms can work out with their kids and see other moms. We work out with the stroller. We walk or jog and then do exercises like lunges and squats. We may do push-ups at a park picnic table or triceps dips at the bench. Moms get a total body workout all while singing to their kids and having fun with other moms.

Apparently I wasn't the only one looking for that connection, because my little idea took off. Within two years, we became a franchise. Two decades later, we have hundreds of franchisees and thousands of instructors nationwide. We grew to be a company providing fitness for every stage of motherhood with eight different pre- and postnatal programs. The business took off through "word of mom" and through big media exposure like *The Today Show, Good Morning America*, and so much more.

I created a multi-million dollar business, starred in fitness DVDs, and became a speaker and author. I had a great marriage and two wonderful kids. I had figured out how to be successful through goal setting and habit building; yet something was still missing. My life felt frenetic. I was caught up in a whirlwind of chaos and distraction, where I was always chasing the next goal. I started this business so I could be a mom first and foremost, but running a nationwide franchise became overwhelming. I never felt like I was doing anything good enough, not motherhood, entrepreneurship, or marriage. I definitely wasn't doing a good job taking care of myself. I muddled through each day of burnout and knew there had to be something better out there. Yes, I knew how to get things done through my strategy of breaking things down, but I was missing peace. I was missing joy. I found myself living for weekends and vacations and just hustling through each week day. I knew how to create a strategy and break down big goals; but I was missing how to live the life I desired.

Success leaves clues. I had coached thousands of women and interviewed dozens for my articles and podcasts. Through this work, it became very clear what wasn't working (multi-tasking, rushing, and over-commitment) and what was (mindfulness, meditation, gratitude, and play).

I remember the day I had an "epipha-ME." I realized that my overfull chaotic life had been designed by me. I created it, which meant I could also *uncreate* it. I sat down with a sheet of paper and got clear on what was most important to me. I redesigned my life. I applied what I knew about goal setting and breaking down goals to life habits and joy. Within our modern culture, it is a universal wish to be happy, but this desire for happiness can lead to *destination addiction*, causing many of us to suffer while trying to achieve it. The gap between myself and happiness was my own doing. I realized that my stress and time famine were of my own creation, and it was up to me to find my way out of it. It was time to start appreciating the micro moments of living. Living is what we do every day when we wake up, go to work, parent our kids, and wash the dishes. Living is what happens between the big celebrations and memory moments like vacations and birthday parties and weddings. Those seemingly mundane activities can bring joy and appreciation into your life.

So I created a system to help me find joy and purpose each day. As a CEO, we use systems to track goals and metrics to make sure we are on track. KPIs are key performance indicators. They are numbers that we watch in business to make sure we are on the right track. Most CEOs create a dashboard to make sure you are moving in the right direction. You can't try to track everything, so you focus on what's most important at that time. Think of the dashboard of your car. It could show you one hundred different things going on in your car; but that would be too much to focus on. Instead, your car's dashboard shows about four to seven things: tachometer, speed, gas, oil, temperature, and maybe the electric charge.

I created a similar process for my life. Because I have ADD and it is easy for me to try to do too much, I focused on just a few important things at a time. I have been doing this for a very long time, so the habits have compounded into a very successful and fulfilling life. It is a daily process to ground me in the energy that I want in my day; it is a check-in to remind me of what is important and to help me focus each day. This ritual sets the tone for my day. I calm my monkey brain through journaling and set my intention on who I want to be and how I want to be. I became clear on what was most important to me and designed my days to make sure those things came first. I pruned out things that were making me feel too full. My system didn't cost money. My system didn't need a coach or course. It just required mindset and habit.

Sustained now for over a decade, this system changed my life. Without a doubt, I am happier and more at peace now than I ever was before. I found my way out of burnout and into a grateful and joyful life. All the while, I was still parenting two kids and running a national business.

I have broken my practice down into small steps to take each day. I want to help you find joy and purpose in each and every day. While we wish life would change in a quantum leap, it is more likely to change through small steps inching us forward every day. The idea is to orient yourself correctly in the direction of the life you want to live.

Before we jump into my system, let's get connected to my mindset on all of this.

LEVEL UP FOR JOY

Most people want to be happy, yet few manage to achieve it. The pursuit of happiness often leads to *destination addiction*, or the notion that happiness is tied to achieving a certain thing—job, marriage, body, vacation, _____. You can fill in the blank. I thought I would be happy when I took off the baby weight. When I went on vacation. I kept telling Jason, "I'll be happy when I get through this next project."

"No," he said. "When you get through this next project, you will just take on another one."

And he was right. With your happiness based on outside factors, you soon realize that happiness is never where you are. It becomes impossible to enjoy the present. Happiness is always being deferred.

We often try to achieve happiness through pleasure. For example, we eat pleasurable foods, watch a favorite show, or drink an alcoholic beverage of choice. While pleasure can be enjoyable and can provide temporary positive feelings, it does not necessarily lead to long-term happiness.

JOY VERSUS PLEASURE

When we feel low, we often seek pleasure. Pleasure can come in the form of watching a show, having a glass of wine, shopping, eating... the list goes on. What's your favorite form of pleasure? There's nothing wrong with that, except that it is fleeting. The show ends. The glass of wine empties. The item we shopped for loses its excitement. And then we are left without again. I am certainly not saying pleasure is bad; I am just aware that some pleasures leave me feeling emptier than when I began.

The other challenge of pleasure seeking is that it just leads to wanting more. To combat my stress and unhappiness, I sought more pleasure. I would give myself pleasure through food, alcohol, watching a favorite show, shopping. I found that pleasure can often be fleeting and short-lived. The enjoyment of a pleasurable experience may fade quickly, leaving you with a sense of emptiness or dissatisfaction. This can lead to a constant need for more pleasure, which can become a cycle of seeking immediate gratification without ever achieving long-term satisfaction or happiness. I am not discounting pleasure; however, I am encouraging you not to use pleasure to escape or numb or distract yourself from life.

Instead of seeking pleasure, I started to seek joy. Joy is a deeper and more profound emotion that can arise from a sense of connection, purpose, and meaning in life. Pursuing momentary pleasures or material possessions may bring temporary happiness, but they do not lead to sustained joy.

Joy brings a sense of fulfillment. Pursuing joy often involves engaging in activities that align with one's values and interests, leading to a sense of fulfillment and satisfaction. This can contribute to a more meaningful and purposeful life.

Joy strengthens relationships. Pursuing joy often involves

connecting with others and fostering meaningful relationships, which can enhance social support and contribute to a greater sense of well-being.

Joy encourages personal growth. Pursuing joy often involves taking on challenges and engaging in activities that promote personal growth, leading to a greater sense of self-awareness and self-improvement.

Pursuing joy can lead to a more fulfilling and meaningful life, while pursuing pleasure alone may lead to a focus on momentary satisfaction or external achievements that do not bring sustained well-being.

I have achieved contentment through new perspective and purpose in my life. I have pleasure through gratitude and appreciation for the nuances of my life. It's a relief to let go of the pursuit of happiness and to instead be at peace with the life I have created for myself. This is what I want to share. Imagine finding joy in your simple, everyday life.

The big message of this book is that joy comes from appreciating the experience of living your life. Joy is making the most out of each year, each month, each day, each moment. It's about living on purpose, so you don't just *get through* life's in-between moments. It's about building habits that help you live your best life. Ask anyone who has lived a long life, and they will tell you that it happens in the blink of an eye. They will tell you that they wish they had slowed down and enjoyed the little moments more. The joy of living is an appreciation of the good with the bad, the celebrations and the times between.

EMBRACING THE STRUGGLE

One thing that kept me from my joy was my utter discomfort in struggle. Yes, of course struggle is supposed to be uncomfortable.

But I ran from being uncomfortable like it was the plague. I was constantly trying to keep my life away from hard things, hard conversations, hard feelings. The challenge in always seeking happiness is that you feel incredibly unhappy when you encounter struggles. And the thing is, you will encounter struggle. Life is frickin' hard. It is not a curated Instagram feed. It's messy. I wish I had learned as a child to approach struggles head-on as an opportunity. I wish I hadn't expected or dreamt that life would look like a Disney fairytale.

Pinterest, Instagram, Home Edit, and Marie Kondo are constantly showing us how perfect everyone else's lives look. We scroll through a photoshopped, curated, edited world and feel like failures when we don't have our own perfectly happy and beautiful life. Our kids pose as influencers online, but they live in a real, hard, unfiltered world. How will it feel for them when they realize their own life experiences do not match the illusion online?

When faced with discomfort or struggle, we want to mask it, avoid it, or numb it. But escapism via alcohol, drugs, or food doesn't work. Instead, we find ourselves in a new pandemic of anxiety, depression, and mental health challenges. We are not prepared for discomfort. I don't know that you will find joy in the discomfort, but you can find growth, opportunity, and purpose in it, and through those things you will achieve joy long-term.

I have come to realize that without challenges, there is no growth. In fitness, we talk a lot about getting comfortable with being uncomfortable. That is where the transformation happens. This is true in all of life. It's funny, I never minded hard work—I just minded hard human interactions. I shied away from tough conversations with my parents, my sister, my husband, my friends, and my employees because I didn't like the discomfort of conflict. When I learned how to face these conversations, my relationships became so much richer. In my younger years, I avoided all struggle. I didn't work hard in school or sports or pretty much anything. I was missing the best parts of my life because I didn't want to be uncomfortable. I had to learn that getting uncomfortable was the only way I could live my best life.

BUDDHISM AND SUFFERING

I took a World Religions class in college and was intrigued by the Buddhist philosophy. That interest has prompted me to read much about the teachings. Buddhist doctrine states that suffering, illness, and death are to be expected, understood, and acknowledged. Fear and uncertainty are natural to ordinary life. Part of making peace with our reality is expecting impermanence and embracing lack of control and unpredictability. To think that things should be otherwise only adds unnecessary suffering. Where there is no suffering, there is no happiness or joy. The opposite is also true.

Perhaps it's time to stop trying to feel good and instead learn to be good at feeling. Instead of running from your feelings, you must confront them to realize you are okay. For example, I have suffered from migraines in recent years. One meditation technique for dealing with the pain is to go right into it. Feel it, and then it will release.

THOUGHTS

Your stinking thinking may be robbing you of your joy. According to the National Science Foundation, we have 60,000 thoughts per day. Ninety-eight percent of them are the same thoughts you had yesterday. And I'm guessing most of those thoughts are not serving you. You see a car commercial and think, *I need that car to be happy.* You scroll through Instagram and think, *I need that style to be happy.* You see a house on Pinterest and think, *I need that home to be happy.* But none of these thoughts bring you happiness. They just distract you.

You don't need any external things—you need to unplug and rewire your brain. And you can. Neuroplasticity is the brain's ability to reorganize itself. Your brain can be trained, much like a muscle. Habits can strengthen your brain. For instance, a habit of daily affirmations can train the brain to focus on the positive. Similarly, a habit of having a do-over thought when you have a negative thought will help extinguish the unwanted thought spiral.

Our brains are naturally hardwired to focus on the bad and discard the good. It's called negativity bias, and it's a protective mechanism that prioritizes danger avoidance over a focus on the positive. Examples are how we remember insults more than compliments. We dwell on traumatic events more than positive ones. We notice our imperfections more than our perfections. The problem is, negative thoughts beget more negative thoughts; they become even more deeply ingrained in our brain's wiring. But there is good news: We can rewire our brains through new habits. We can create new neural connections by intentionally creating new thought patterns.

An example of such a habit is to do a do-over thought. When you have a negative thought, first be aware of it, and then create a new thought to replace it. For example, I need to do a do-over thought when my alarm goes off in the am. My alarm goes off at 5:00 a.m. every morning. When I hear that alarm, it's so easy to reflexively think, *Why can't I sleep in?*, or, *Ugh, I'm tired.* I'm sure you have your own version. So when that negative thought pops in my head (and it does), I make myself think a do-over thought. For instance, *I will have so much more time for myself by getting up at this hour*, or, *I will be so happy that I got up early.* Or simply, *Coffee*.

WILLPOWER, MOTIVATION, AND HABITS

How many of us wish we had more willpower? I'm raising my hand along with you. We wish we had more willpower to resist dessert, to curb our phone scrolling, to decline that second glass of wine. Or perhaps we believe we need more motivation? Maybe we should be more motivated to rise early for a workout or to adhere to our diet? Motivation and willpower, we're told, are the keys to success. We chase after them, hoping they'll sustain us through our goals; yet, despite our efforts, they often falter, leaving us feeling frustrated and defeated.

I once met a personal trainer who worked with stars like Madonna and Tom Hanks. I asked him what his secret was to get them in such great shape. He said it wasn't his secret; it was their motivation. They knew they would be on a big screen baring their abs, and then they were very motivated to get results. The celeb trainer Tony Horton once said that if you are only motivated to lose weight for an upcoming wedding, you better have a lot of weddings to go to. The challenge with motivation is that it's not always there. You might be motivated to lose weight, but you are more motivated to eat tacos with your friends. Maybe the truth is that it doesn't mean that much to you. If it did, you would do it.

But what if there's another way? What if, instead of relying solely on fleeting motivation and fragile willpower, we focused on something more enduring? Enter habits. Unlike motivation and willpower, habits are like sturdy pillars supporting our actions. They're the autopilot mode of our behavior, guiding us effortlessly through our daily routines. Building habits means embedding desired actions into our subconscious, making them almost second nature. By cultivating habits, we lessen the need for constant motivation and willpower, allowing us to navigate life with greater ease and consistency. So let's shift our focus away from chasing elusive motivation and bolstering fragile willpower, and instead invest our energy in building habits that will carry us steadily toward our goals.

How long does it take to build a habit? Most often, I hear twenty-one days. That is actually inaccurate. The truth is that it depends on the habit you ware wanting to break or create. Some take less time and some take more. The average time is probably closer to sixty-six days. You know something is a habit when it becomes automatic, when you don't need motivation or willpower to achieve it. My suggestion is that you do less and really conquer those habits. Let's say you choose to work on two to three new habits each month. Some may take a little longer than others. That is about twelve to eighteen new habits in a year. What would your life look like with twelve to eighteen new habits?

Here is a sampling from my own list of habits:

- Wake up at 5:00 a.m.
- Drinks 64 ounces of water
- Walk the dogs daily
- Read two books per month
- Exercise six days per week
- Journal five days per week
- Meditate five days per week
- Ice plunge three days per week
- Reticular Activating System five days per week

- Balance exercises five days per week
- Morning start-up ritual
- Morning shutdown ritual
- Monthly date night
- Monthly hike with friends
- Monthly game night with friends
- Write book five days per week
- Quarterly unplugged day
- Annual planning

My point in sharing this is that I didn't achieve this in a single week, month, or even year. I have been building up these habits for a very long time. What am I working on now?

- Taking vitamins daily
- Meal planning one day per week
- Balance training five days per week
- No alcohol five days per week
- Foam Rolling nightly before bed

BABY STEPS
I told you earlier that the way I dealt with my ADD was to break things down into baby steps. When anything felt too overwhelming, I would break it into the smallest step that felt doable. Well, this works amazingly with your habits. Have you ever heard of the one push-up challenge? The one push-up challenge is a fitness challenge where individuals aim to do just one push-up. It might sound easy, but the challenge often encourages people who are less active or just starting with fitness to engage in physical activity. It can serve as a gateway to building healthier habits, as even one push-up can be a

significant accomplishment for some people. In this book, we are going to build new habits that will Level Up your life. If any habit feels too big, then chunk it down.

LET'S GET STARTED
In this book, I share the system I have created. I bring together my experience from my master's in psychology, my experience as a CEO and business owner, my learnings from coaches and mentors, wisdom from Buddhist doctrine, lessons from the hundreds of women I have interviewed, and much personal experimentation. I want to teach you how to be the CEO of your life. We'll start with getting realigned with what is most important in your life. We will figure out which parts of your life need more attention and which parts need less.

I bring my process to life with the Level Up Journal so you can record your progress as you incorporate the practices into your daily life. The journal system includes prompts for goal setting, free writing, and tracking. Each day, you give yourself scores for where you are in your life, relationships, health. The concept is to focus in and Level Up where you want to in your life.

The Level Up Journal can be used to track any aspect of your life. The concept is to choose a habit that you want to focus on. What I share with you are the habits that I have built to find more joy and meaning in my life. Each chapter in this book is dedicated to a different focus, helping you decide where and how to Level Up, and finishes with ideas for habits that can be added to daily life and tracked in the Level Up Journal.

Designing the life you want is quite simple. Putting principles into practice isn't always as easy. But shifting your mindset takes one baby step at a time. And I'm here to walk you through every step of the way.

WHAT LEVEL IS YOUR LIFE?

"For a successful life, or successful business,
measure what you want to improve."

– JERRY BRUCKNER

I'm a little embarrassed to show you behind the curtain of my crazy, but I believe our weird quirks are also our gifts. Before I give you a look, though, let me tell you how I got here. I shared in the Introduction that I lived a life of "can't" when I was a child. I had ADD. I was unorganized, unmotivated, and unsocial. After that incident where I was held up at gunpoint, I started to change my life. I started putting effort in, making baby steps to where I wanted to go. Progress added up day after day, year after year. I became successful by most accounts. In school. With friends. Then in business. But as a young mom, juggling a national business and two young children, I felt empty. Out of control. Overwhelmed. The list goes on. I was in magazines and on national television, but I wasn't feeling successful in life. It seemed like everyone felt this way. I barely had time to question it.

I remember one phone conversation with my sister where she said, "This is out of control. You started this business so you could be a mom first and foremost. You are so busy that you don't have time for anyone, including yourself." It was tough love. But a sister will hold up a mirror that you won't hold up for yourself. Thank you, Kim. That moment changed everything. I realized that I had created this mess and it was up to me to create something different.

I sat down with a sheet of paper and got clear on what was most important to me. I started to re-design my life. Now, I realize that we all want change to happen in a quantum leap. It doesn't happen like that. It happens by stacking small daily habits on top of each other. It happens from being focused on what you want and don't want in your life. It happens when you stick with it. The tools that I am sharing in this chapter have been cultivated for more than a decade. They continue to iterate. My suggestion as you go through the book is that you do just a little at a time, but you commit to it consistently.

I have created a process for living my life on purpose. As a CEO, I have had to establish extensive structures for how to plan each year and accomplish the company's goals. In business, we have tools and structure. A <u>good</u> business typically does the following:

- Has a vision and is clear on the "why"
- Has a mission statement
- Has a business plan
- Does a SWOT analysis (Strengths, Weaknesses, Opportunities, Threats)
- Has KPIs (key performance indicators) to make sure you are staying on track

- Annual reviews / annual planning
- Does quarterly check-ins to make sure business is moving towards plan

I had mastered all of this in my business. I figured that would work in my own life—and it has.

We are so busy that we rarely take the time to work on our lives. That changes now. Your life is precious, and it is deserving of thoughts and plans. Your life is worth working on. Your life is worth creating plans and goals and strategies. Your life is worth checking in on. When we are off track in business, we make adjustments. The same goes for your life. Here is how to bring this to life in your life.

ANNUALLY

In my business, we go on an annual planning retreat once a year to create the plan for the year ahead. In my life, I set aside time as well. Maybe not a retreat, but definitely some purposeful time.

The Annual Check-In consists of three activities:

1. Most Important Things (MITs)
2. Wheel of Life
3. Have. Do. Be.

My suggestion is to jot down notes of what bubbles up for you as you read this book. Right now, you might not have any idea what you want in your life. That's okay. As you read on, you will start to get some clarity on what you want to focus on. When you are done with the book, take a little time to work on your plan. After that, revisit it on a yearly basis. I like to do mine the week before the start of a new year—I find the week after the winter holidays to be slower, and I'm usually off work, but that's just me! You pick any time. It doesn't have to be an annual January to December calendar. Perhaps your year starts right now, when you are reading this book. What matters most is that you block some time to review the year and plan what you want to create the following year. The following three activities will help you do this.

I suggest grabbing a blank journal that will keep all of these activities for the year. This is *your* Level Up Journal. I have dozens of these journals, and it's amazing to go back and see how my life has grown and what I've learned.

Ideally, get out of your usual physical space. Go to a space that feels good, that inspires you. This could be a coffee shop, a co-working space, a park. When you change your surroundings, you can shift your outlook and your perspective. This part is not required; I have done it many times in my home. I just find that ideas flow more freely when you change up your setting a bit. I do encourage you to block out some quiet time for this. Your big idea will never happen when you are busy. And it's hard to get creative when you have TV in the background, kids in your ear, and the dog at your feet. You are the CEO of your life. The CEO should have some quiet space! I am providing you with some activities that you will do annually, quarterly, monthly and daily.

ACTIVITY 1: MOST IMPORTANT THINGS (MITS)

I mentioned above that as a new business owner and a new mom that I found myself drowning in overwhelm. I was trying to keep up with running a national business and raising my kids. I felt like nothing I did was good enough. When I had that "epipha-ME," I decided enough was enough and decided to redesign my life. I realized that my to-do list was a mile long and none of the things on it were really important to me. I was living out of alignment with what I valued. I needed to get clarity on what was important to me.

I took out a sheet of paper and made three intersecting circles. I needed to get clear on what was most important to me, because I couldn't focus on everything. It's hard to pick just three things. So many things are important to us. The first time I did this, I wrote down "Family," "Friends," and "Business." But that didn't feel right. Whatever energy I had was being put in the business and my kids. My marriage was being neglected. So, I changed it. I put "Marriage," "Business," and "Kids." Of course, friends were still important to me. But if I needed to choose how I was going to invest my time, I was purposefully choosing my marriage over my friends.

Side note: Now that my kids are grown, I have far more time for my friends. Your MITs can change for each season of your life. I needed to create my life and my schedule with these as the first priority. With one caveat: I could not take care of my marriage, my kids, or my business if I didn't take care of myself. I put *me* in the center.

That activity was a pivotal moment and became my North Star for the direction of my life.

Let's figure out your Most Important Things (MITs).

Open up your journal. Write "MITs" on the top of the page. Now, list all of the things that are important to you in your life. Just do a brain dump. Don't judge your list. Don't edit your list. Just empty your heart. What is important to you right now, at this point in your life? If you didn't come up with ten to twenty, keep going; you're not done.

My personal example:

Friends
Family
Home
Health
My Marriage
My Kids
My Dogs
Exercise
Nature
Gardening
Learning / Growth
Good Food
Travel
Time
Coffee
Sleep
Work
Income
Fun
Adventure
Helping Others / Charity
Gratitude
Entertainment
Peace
Speaking
Retreats
Financial Security

Let's do the first edit. Circle the top eight things that are important to you. Don't worry. It doesn't mean the other things aren't important. They can still be part of your life. They are just lower on the priority ladder.

Now the hard part: Pick just three.

How do you know what to pick? Here's a little exercise for you. At the end of your life, what will you regret not spending time on? What advice do you think you would give your younger self? Do not pick what your parents or significant other would want you to do. Choose what feels honoring to your needs and desires right now. If you had time for only three things, what would give you the best life?

I have picked the fourth for you already, and that is *you:* your health, your well-being.

Other things can still be important, but these three things are the compass for your choices. When you live in alignment with your MITs, you will find that life is energy giving and not depleting.

Once you've selected your three MITs, take a look at your calendar or planner. Does the time you spend each day reflect the importance of your three MITs? For most of us, it does not, and that's why we feel out of alignment. Living in alignment with your goals and your purpose is the key that unlocks your joyful life. I will share with you in this book how to block your schedule so these things are the "big rocks."

Stephen Covey popularized the "big rocks" concept. He would take out a jar and fill it with big rocks. It appeared to be full. Then he would fill it with gravel. Now it was full. Then he would fill it with sand. Now, it was surely full. But, finally, he would fill the jar with water. It's a powerful metaphor for prioritizing what's important in our life. If we start with the big rocks first, we can make room for the small stuff. But if you fill your day with the sand and gravel (things like social media, TV, wasting time), you won't have time for what's most important to you.

These MITs should become your North Star, your compass. They drive what's most important to you to spend your time on. The reason you feel out of balance is because you are living out of alignment with your values.

I am going to oversimplify this. Reverse engineer your calendar. What are some things you could do to fulfill these MITs? Go on a monthly date with your spouse? Exercise three days per week? Meal plan once a week? The holy grail is to block out your calendar so there is first room for your MITs. Those are your big rocks. Everything else has to fit on top of them.

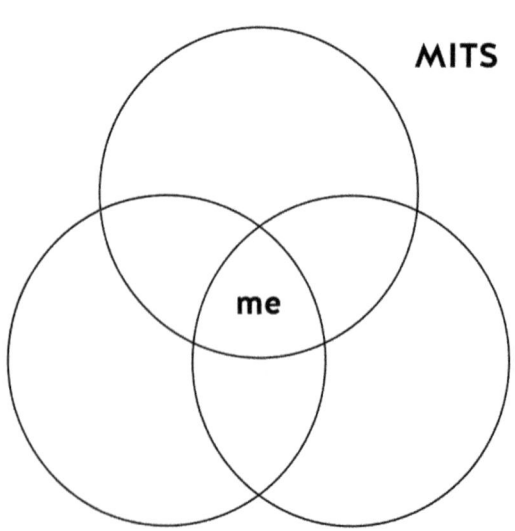

ACTIVITY 2: WHEEL OF LIFE

The next annual activity I do is the Wheel of Life Assessment. I was first introduced to this exercise through Zig Ziglar. I have seen many variations over the years. Zig's premise was that life success came from being balanced in each spoke of the wheel:

Mental
Spiritual
Physical
Family
Financial
Personal
Career

You can put whatever you want into the spokes. What are the areas you want to measure? Choose from above, or here are some other sections I have done…

Marriage
Kids
Fun
Relationships
Personal Growth
Home / Environment

It's a great activity. I have created my own version of this as part of my annual plan.

1. Get out your Journal. Write Wheel of Life at the top.

2. Make a big circle.

3. Divide it up into eight sections.

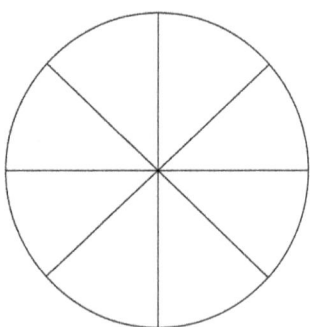

4. Put ten notches on each line, numbered one to ten, starting at the inside.

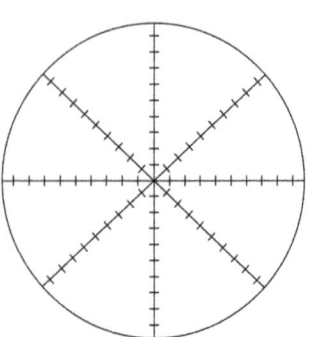

5. Remember when you came up with your list of top eight things that are important in your life? Fill in yours in each of the sections. Or you are welcome to choose one from Zig Ziglar's list.

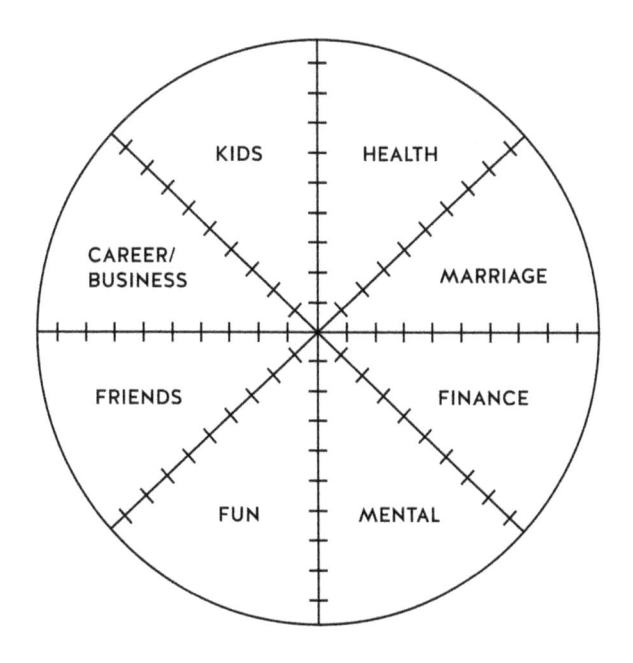

KIDS | HEALTH
CAREER/BUSINESS | MARRIAGE
FRIENDS | FINANCE
FUN | MENTAL

6. Now, it gets interesting. Give yourself a score in each category between one and ten, with ten being best, based on how well you feel you are doing in each category. A ten means you feel absolutely amazing in that category! Of course, they are not absolutes. Just follow your gut. Most importantly, determine which categories score lower or higher than others. Plot your scores in the circle. Make a line that connects where you scored.

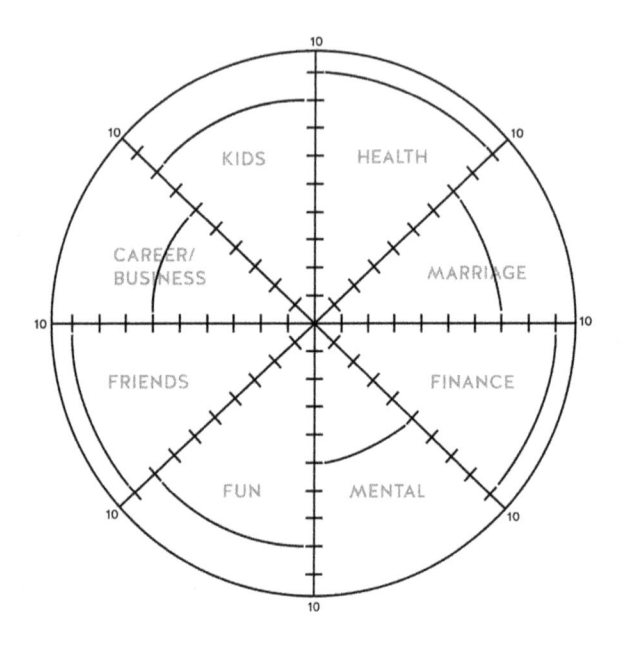

[Wheel of life diagram with eight segments labeled: KIDS, HEALTH, MARRIAGE, FINANCE, MENTAL, FUN, FRIENDS, CAREER/BUSINESS, each spoke marked from 0 to 10.]

A wheel is round, but the spokes on your wheel probably won't be. Once you've filled in the circle, take a few minutes to reflect on how you've scored in each area. You will see that you are stronger in some areas than others.

How do you feel when looking at your scores? Where do you want to see improvement? If you try to change everything, you will probably change nothing. We need to keep editing and focusing on what's most important to us right now. My goal is not to have tens in all areas (although that would be dreamy). My goal is to be in touch with each area of my life and to be accepting of what I'm not ready to change and to be focused where I do want to change. For example, there have been times where I was unhappy with my financial spoke, so I spent time that year educating myself about money and working to improve my savings. There have been times where my friend score is low, and I didn't try to change it because I realized it was a stage of my life where time with friends wasn't as important as other spokes.

In the following chapters, we are going to address many areas that may be on your wheel. You will see how we pick just one or two things to focus on and make them into habits. I use this assessment to help me decide what I need to work on this year.

I now want you to average all of the numbers on your wheel of life. That is your "life score." What level are you living at? Where do you want to be? This is where you Level Up! Choose habits to work on based on where you want to Level Up.

ACTIVITY 3: HAVE. DO. BE.

I have had many coaches and mentors in my life. When I was in a CEO peer group, one of my mentors gave us an exercise to help executives clarify what they want in their life. It works for everyone, and I now do my own version of it every year. I have even shared this activity with my husband. It's pretty eye-opening to see if you both want the same things in life. Open up your journal. Title the page, "Have. Do. Be."

Sit down and give yourself some time to answer the following questions each year. If you don't have answers to these questions, come back to this exercise after reading the book. My guess is that it will give you more clarity about what you want in your life. If you are jumping in now, that's fine. Just give yourself grace if you are unsure about what you want; or keep this exercise in mind as you read the book so you can gain clarity when you are ready to put pen to paper.

Divide up your paper into two columns with three big boxes. An example is below.

	HAVE	**DO**	**BE**
WANT			
DON'T WANT			

What do you want to have in your life?
What do you not want to have in your life?

What do you want to do in your life?
What do you not want to do?

How do you want to be in your life?
How do you not want to be?

Examples from my own Have. Do. Be. List:

What do you want to have?	What do you not want to have?
A new kitchen	Stress
Peace	Debt
A happy marriage	Clutter

What do you want to do?	What do you not want to do?
Organize my sock drawer	Scroll my life on my phone
Meditate daily	Over commit
Make my health a priority	Live in busy
Have time with friends	Drink alcohol during the week
Go on vacation	Fight with my spouse

How do you want to be?	How do you not want to be?
Peaceful	Stressed
Healthy	Chaotic
Focused	Frantic
Loving	Distracted

You can see that the choices are not limited. You can pick material things and non-material things. You can see that there is also overlap with recurring themes. That's okay! Patterns can reveal that a certain topic is particularly important to you.

Finding clarity in the life you desire is the first step. The daily habits we will build together are how you will get there. I go through this exercise every year, and it's pretty cool to look back and see how many of the things I've written down have come to life.

What would need to happen to accomplish the things on my own Have. Do. Be list? What would need to happen to take my marriage to another level? To go swimming with whale sharks? To write a book? Yes, writing this book was on my Have. Do. Be list! What would need to happen to accomplish your own list?

Want to take this a step further? Create a vision board that is guided by your Have. Do. Be. It's an opportunity to dream and explore and design the life you desire. Funny story: I said I wanted to have a new kitchen and put it on my vision board. My husband saw it and said, "Sorry, honey, but I don't see that in the cards this year." Well, our house flooded, and we ended up with a new kitchen! Perhaps we don't always need a plan but just need to trust that the universe will help us get there.

ANNUAL LEVEL UP

Look at your MITs, your wheel of life, and your Have. Do. Be list. What do you want to focus on in the year ahead? Most people try to do too much, too hard, too fast. We try to do everything and end up doing, well, nothing. Pick the areas of your life that are most important to you at this stage of your life. We are building new habits together. Once one thing becomes a habit, you can add more.

If your marriage is an area that you want to Level Up, think of a dozen habits that might help you reach the next level.

Example: My goal is to Level Up my marriage this year. I will do this by:

- Planning a monthly date night
- Reading a marriage book
- Doing a ten-second kiss each day

- Putting my phone down when having a conversation with my spouse

QUARTERLY
Why don't New Year's resolutions work? Well, for one thing, people come up with goals and then forget about them. Plus, a year is just too big of an undertaking. I suggest you break your goals into ninety-day sprints, just like we do in business. Break your goals into smaller chunks. Every goal has multiple steps, and you shouldn't expect to be able to do everything at once. I am all about reverse engineering whatever I want to accomplish into smaller, bite-sized tasks. If it feels too big, break it down further. Don't plan all four quarters at once. Just plan the next quarter. What do you want to focus on in the next quarter? What are small action steps you can take to make progress in the areas that you want to focus on?

In my example above, it is too overwhelming to do all of those things at once. So, instead, break it down into quarterly focuses.

Example: My goal is to Level Up my marriage this year. I will do this by:

- Planning a monthly date night - Q1
- Reading a marriage book - Q2
- Doing a ten-second kiss each day - Q3
- Putting my phone down when having a conversation with my spouse - Q4

If you feel like you can do more, go for it. But isn't it better to truly commit and make a change than to create many goals you don't follow through on?

ACTIVITY: UNPLUGGED DAY

Choose one day every three months to unplug, sit down, and check in on your goals. When you plug in a destination on your GPS, you check in along the way to make sure you are going in the right direction. This is your check-in so you can make adjustments if you are off course.

> Where are you on track?
> Where are you off track?
> Are the goals you set still important to you?

It's a day to work *on* your life instead of *in* it. It's also a day to "unplug" so you can recharge. No meetings, no email, no social media. I go on a run, get out into nature, do yoga, journal. I give myself purposeful space. Because your big a-ha moment will never happen while you're busy—it happens when you have space to daydream. I look forward to these days!

This is when and where I come up with my next quarter's goals. I figure out what I want to focus on for the next few months.

The idea is never to be perfect. My hope is to be directionally correct. Am I moving in the right direction? Go to your calendar and book when you are going to take an Unplugged Day!

MONTHLY

At the beginning of the month, get clear on the habits you want to work on, based on your quarterly goals. I write two to three Level Up goals for that month. These goals should come from your MITs and your quarterly goals. If one of my MI's was my marriage, then I might set a monthly goal to go on a monthly date night. If I set a goal to run a marathon this year, then my monthly goal may be to run four days per week. When I sit down to do my daily journaling, I check in on these goals. Here are some examples of what that might look like.

DAILY
The way I stay grounded to my goals, my values, and my intentions is through my daily journaling process. This is the bulk of your Level Up Journal. It has now evolved into five steps:

- Free Write
- Powerful Questions
- Gratitude
- Habit Tracker
- Affirmations

While this may sound like a lot, it takes me no more than fifteen minutes each day to complete. It has been a gift in my life and grounds me to what I want to create in my life. My hope is that you wake up fifteen minutes earlier to do this exercise. Of course, it could be done any time in the day. But a morning ritual is a great way to ground yourself and set the tone for your day. You are getting "mind-right" and steering your brain for the direction you want to take for the day.

ACTIVITY 1: FREE WRITE (ALSO KNOWN AS JOURNALING)
Here, I simply write down the date and get thoughts out of my head and onto paper. At first, the idea of journaling did not appeal to me, but one of my writer friends urged me to start nearly two decades ago. I didn't feel like I could be honest about my deepest feelings or thoughts if I was concerned that someone would read it. What I have found to be true is

completely different than that. My journal is just a place to untangle my thoughts. It's a brain dump. I usually start with what's weighing on my mind. What's challenging me. What's working. What I have figured out. What was a win from the previous day? Sometimes it's a few lines. Sometimes it's a full paragraph. It is fascinating to look back at old journals and see how long we deal with the same issues. This practice is what ignited the practice that I now share with you.

ACTIVITY 2: POWERFUL QUESTIONS

After I free write, I ask myself a powerful question. I once saw author Marshall Goldsmith speak about the power of daily questions. He said this one single practice could transform your life, so I tried it and added it to my routine. He was right. Powerful questions lead to powerful thoughts and purposeful days. It's a practice I value, so now I complete my journal entry by asking myself one question each day. Some of the questions include…

How am I alive today?
Who do I want to be today?
How will I do 1 percent better today?
How can I respond instead of react today?
What's most important to me today?
How can I show the people I love that I love them today?
How do I want to help someone today?
How will I move towards my goals?
How will I find meaning in my day?

The act of choosing which question I'm going to answer gets my brain flowing on my desire and energy for the day. I sit with them a moment and reflect what's bubbling up for me. These questions ground me to what's important and to my purpose for the day. The answers help organize my thoughts and how I want to live my day.

ACTIVITY 3: GRATITUDE

Each morning, I list everything I am thankful for. I challenge myself to think of something new that I haven't given thanks for before, or I try to think of something specific that happened the day before. There are so many little things we take for granted. The daily practice of thinking of things we are grateful for deepens our gratitude for each day. I believe so much in the power of gratitude, that there is a whole chapter ahead on it!

I am grateful for my health, family, home, friends, food and water, peace, kindness, work, income, safety, freedom, my dogs, warmth, comfort, shoes, nature, free time.

ACTIVITY 4: LEVEL UP HABIT TRACKER

Ask any CEO, and they will tell you that they have a dashboard or data sheet that tracks their KPIs (key performance indicators). They track what's most important to them. They check in regularly to make sure they are on track and can make adjustments as needed. Why should your life be any different? It's not about being perfect. I have no room for self-loathing or feeling like I'm not good enough right now. We all get off track. My commitment to myself is growth. This habit tracker will help you connect to what's important and get back in alignment with the life you want to live.

This section of the journal is your Level Up game changer. You will create a graph like the one below to track your habits.

This is where you track the habits that will tie to your MITs, including your health goals. This is where we track the habits you committed to. If you are wanting to run a marathon, then we are going to track the habit of running. You might track your water intake or your meditations. As a CEO, I love data. I find that what you measure gets better. I also add some other daily notes about how I'm feeling and doing, and when I compare my habits with my feelings, it becomes apparent how my habits are correlated with my well-being.

As I mentioned earlier in the book, I have ADD and a monkey mind that hasn't always served me. I didn't always follow through on my desired goals, whether it was fitness or nutrition—or anything, really. I found I did much better when I honed in on just a few key habits, checked in on them daily, and committed to checking off the boxes. Our brain loves to check a box. We get a dopamine hit each time we check or cross off a to-do list item. That reward makes us want to do it again. Charles Duhigg, author of *The Power of Habit*, talks about a three-step habit loop: Cue, Routine, and Reward.

Here is an example: Let's say you want to develop the habit of exercising in the morning. You can set up a *cue* for yourself by leaving out your workout clothes the night before. The *routine* is the workout. If you are lucky, you feel the reward of working out right away. But the *reward* is rarely instantaneous. You brush your teeth, and you instantly feel the reward of a fresh mouth. But you floss your teeth, and the reward of healthy gums is less tangible. The reward of working out to achieve weight loss, for example, won't be felt for quite some time after the habit of a nutrition or exercise change. That's where the habit tracker comes in. When you give yourself a "gold star," or in my case, a green box, you are rewarding your brain. The brain gets the dopamine hit it craves from achieving the routine. It's why we all love checking off a task on our to-do list.

As you see those checkmarks build, you get a feeling of reinforcement. Jerry Seinfeld's method for writing jokes is quite similar. Every day that he writes a joke, he puts a big red X on the calendar. His goal is, "Don't break the chain." Much like Jerry, I suggest you track habits that will bring joy into your life. Unlike a hard diet or fitness regime, making slow but steady progress on these habits is going to feel good.

Personally, I use a green colored pencil when I do the habit and a red one when I don't. If you use a journal that's made of graph paper, you can just fill in the box. Otherwise, I draw it out. After tracking for a few weeks, patterns become incredibly apparent. I can see my mood dips when I skip exercise. I can see that I get migraines when I drink alcohol. I can see that my "relationship rating" is lower the week before my period. I see in the data how good I feel when I'm getting enough sleep, making good food choices, and choosing joy.

Here is a list of the habits I currently track. They change depending on the season of life I am in. I am _NOT_ saying that these are the things you should track. These are just the ones that are foundational to me. You need to figure out what's foundational for you.

WF (Whole Foods): I give myself a checkmark if I had an overall good whole food eating day. This is not a nutrition book, so I won't dive deeply here, but I try to stay away from processed foods.

Alc (Alcohol): I note if I drank alcohol. I suffer from migraines, so I know it's something I have to be careful about.

Sug (Sugar): I like to pay attention to keep processed sugars in moderation.

WO (Workouts): I track that I worked out and what workouts I did.

Med (Meditation): You would think that I don't need to track this since it has become a habit, but it's very reinforcing for me to see that I do it regularly.

Sleep: I use a sleep app and note what rating I got on my sleep each night.

I also check in on how I'm feeling in various areas of my life. I start to see trends in how I'm feeling tied to the habits I'm working on.

Moods: I give myself a 1-10 rating on my mood. This is important. I note how the rest might impact how I feel.

♥ (Relationship Rating): I rate on a scale 1-10 how I'm feeling in my relationship with my husband.

Health: I rate on a scale of 1 - 10 on how I'm feeling about my health.

Periods: I track when I get my period. I have been known to be incredibly moody and prone to migraines before my period, so it's helpful to be aware of my cycle.

You will likely have totally different things that you would want to track, and it's totally fine to change them up as your own goals and interests change. Go back to your MITs and the big goals you set. When you get clear on what you are trying to create in your life, you can figure out the habits that will get you there. I have tracked mileage for runs and how much time I have spent writing my book. Heck, if we are really sharing, I have even tracked sex. It just depends on what's important to you at any given time in your life.

Don't put something on your Habit Tracker because you think you should or you see others doing it. What will the benefit be to you? To your family? To those around you? If it's negligible, it's not worth your energy.

I encourage you to track two to five Level Up habits each day. At the end of each chapter, I'll share ideas for things you can try. But keep in mind: If you commit to everything, you commit to nothing. I would rather you commit to less and actually do it. For example, you might start out by committing to documenting gratitude daily, going on a hike weekly, and volunteering once a quarter. Habits don't have to be daily. I have been doing this for years, and I don't have a single month that's "all green." Heck, I rarely have a single week that's all green. It's not about perfection. It's just data. It's about learning and growth. You also don't need to decide now. You haven't even read the whole book!

The best part is, when you track actions for long enough, they become habits and no longer need to be tracked. For example, I don't need to track my daily water intake of 64 ounces anymore because I trained myself to naturally drink enough water each day. I don't need to track taking my vitamins anymore because it's become a habit. I don't track dog walks because it's now a habit.

There are many digital trackers out there, but it's my hope that you put pen to paper. Something happens when we put pen to paper. It boosts your brain's activity and increases your comprehension and creativity. But hey, you do you. You are your own experiment.

ACTIVITY 5: AFFIRMATIONS

I finish my morning Level Up ritual by reading a list of affirmations I have written for myself. Affirmations are sentences aimed to affect the conscious and the subconscious mind. Advertisers spend billions of dollars getting their messages in front of you. They use their messages to convince you that drinking their beverage will make you happy or driving their car will make you sexy. You have control over what's in front of you. So read powerful statements. Affirmations, like prayer, can change the brain at a cellular level. So where do you start? A simple start is to just create "I am" statements. What do you want to be or feel after "I am"?

I am strong.
I am smart.
I am a good person.
I am present.
I am thoughtful.
I am kind.

Here is another powerful technique to figure out your affirmations: Create a list of your five top insecurities. You have to scrape the bottom of your toxic thoughts for this one. It's not comfortable. Then, rewrite them and flip the script so they are powerful and positive. Here are some examples:

I am worthless to everyone. > I am valuable beyond measure.
I am fat and out of shape. > I am healthy and full of possibilities.
I am stupid and lazy. > I am smart and purposeful.

Read the list of the first sentences to yourself. How did that feel? Now read the second set. How did that feel?

What do you think would happen if you read positive, powerful statements to yourself every day? What if you told yourself that you are strong, capable, smart, successful? What if you fed your mind with "I am" and "I can" statements? I will tell you what will happen: Your subconscious mind will start to believe you.

You might be asking, "When the heck do I do this? And how long does it take?" It takes about fifteen minutes of my day, if that. I am a huge proponent of a morning ritual. I'll tell you more about mine later in this book. I always suggest waking up before your family wakes up. I wake up about an hour before my family does. My morning ritual includes this Level Up Journal followed by meditation. And of course there's coffee. It is my best hour of the day. It is how I am able to start the day on my terms and set my own energy. Of course, you can decide what works best for you. These activities could easily be done as an end of day shutdown ritual as well.

This book is about adding habits. This daily journal is the first habit you need to add to your life. What will be your cue to remind you to do it? Don't beat yourself up for when you don't do it, when you get off track, when you don't follow through on a habit. You have no room in your life for that kind of judgment. What is the lesson? How can you learn from it? How can you adjust to do better next time? You just need a few minutes daily to reinforce and remind you what's important to you. It grounds you in what you want to focus on. Now, let's Level Up your life!

You can easily apply my strategy for familiar goals in business and health. But my purpose here is to teach you how to find peace, joy, presence, and connection in your daily life. Little by little, a little becomes a lot.

Throughout the rest of this book, I share the areas that have truly Leveled Up my life. You can Level Up health, finance, etc. There are plenty of books out there that will give you ideas for habits to change. The ones that I am going to share will Level Up your joy of living your life. They will give you insight into how I live on purpose, and how you can too!

GROUNDED IN GRATITUDE

"Gratitude is the healthiest of all human emotions. The more you express gratitude for what you have, the more likely you will have even more to express gratitude for."

– ZIG ZIGLAR

I know what you're thinking: not another platitude about gratitude! Hey, that rhymes. Gratitude is talked about so often and in so many places that it seems redundant.

But the reason it is talked about so often and in so many places is because it truly is that powerful. While gratitude might sound like a cliché, its potency lies in its simplicity. It's not just about feeling thankful; it's about ingraining gratitude as a habit in our lives. Gratitude acts as a catalyst for positive change, enhancing not only our mental but also our physical well-being.

A true practice of gratitude is more than a feeling; it is a habit. In all habits, when you have practiced something over and over, it becomes automatic. You don't have to think about it. The more you do it, the more you train your brain to move in that direction. When you practice, you are essentially building a superhighway in your brain so that the activity becomes more automatic. I can't think of any area of my life where I have experienced this as much as gratitude. A gratitude habit will increase your health, well-being, sleep, and more.

I will share with you some of the habits I use to bring gratitude into my daily life.

Gratitude has several physiological benefits; one reason it's good for you is its impact on the brain's chemistry. When you experience feelings of gratitude, your brain releases neurotransmitters such as dopamine and serotonin, which are associated with pleasure, mood regulation, and overall well-being.

These neurotransmitters not only make you feel good in the moment but also have long-term effects on your brain's health. For instance, dopamine is involved in motivation and reward pathways, so when you feel grateful, it reinforces behaviors associated with gratitude, making you more likely to experience it again.

Moreover, serotonin plays a role in mood stabilization and contributes to feelings of happiness and satisfaction. By fostering a sense of gratitude, you can increase your serotonin levels, which can help alleviate symptoms of depression and anxiety.

Additionally, gratitude activates the hypothalamus, which regulates stress. When these areas are activated, they lead to a reduction in stress hormones like cortisol, resulting in lower stress levels and a more relaxed state of mind.

Overall, the physiological effects of gratitude on the brain contribute to improved mental health, resilience to stress, and a greater sense of well-being.

Before we dive into strategies for cultivating gratitude, let's take a moment to understand what gratitude truly means. At its core, gratitude is about acknowledging and appreciating the good things in life, both big and small. It's about shifting our focus from what we lack to what we have, from complaints to blessings, from negativity to positivity.

START AND END THE DAY WITH GRATITUDE

I mentioned earlier that I wake up very early and often need to do a "do-over thought." In this case, my habit is to start my day with gratitude. When the alarm goes off, I think of one thing I am grateful for. The easiest and most obvious is that I am grateful to be alive to start another day. Someone once told me that every day you wake up above the ground is a good day. It's a privilege denied to many. It sets my mind up to focus on the positive and to start my day with appreciation.

Part of my morning ritual is to write in my journal a list of things I'm thankful for. Each day, I look to add something I have never given thanks for before. For example, have you given thanks for…

- Not having a hangnail?
- The fluffy blanket on your bed?
- Your lungs that breathe, your liver that cleanses, your muscles that move you?
- Having shoes to put on your feet?
- Not being cold or hot?
- The sun to shine each day?
- Not having a tooth ache?

As you explore new things, you also recognize all of the other areas in your life to be grateful for.

When I go to sleep, I don't count sheep. I have created a practice (a habit) of going to sleep thinking of all the things I am grateful for. My health, my marriage, my family, my home. I go on and on until… I fall peacefully asleep. It works every time.

MEET CHALLENGES WITH GRATITUDE

I spoke in the introduction that suffering is a part of life. Let's take it a step further. You should meet challenges not only with acceptance, but with gratitude. As I am writing this chapter, I am in the depths of a heavy challenge in my business. Like the kind of weight that takes up every second of your mental bandwidth, even when I'm sleeping. It sucks. It feels awful. I can easily spiral to despair. But… I am adjusting my mindset. *How is this challenge an opportunity? What is the gift in it?*

Every single day, we encounter challenges. From work problems to toddler tantrums to traffic to teenagers, hard stuff happens. One of the most powerful paradigm shifts for me has been to think about ,"How is this happening *for* me?" instead of, "How is this happening *to* me?" I'm not saying it's easy, but I do think there is a gift in just about any situation if you look for it—and where there is a gift, there is an opportunity for gratitude. When stuck in traffic, I remind myself to be grateful that I have a car and a good podcast to listen to. When I open my email to five hundred unread messages, I think about how amazing it is that five hundred people want to connect with me (well, probably three hundred people, and the rest are spam). When my kids are being difficult, I think about how lucky I am to be in this moment with them—because one day soon, I will miss them.

I am not (I repeat, *I am not*) saying I don't have a negative reaction to these things, nor do I expect you to never have a negative reaction to these things. I get annoyed at the traffic and my kids just like anyone else. But I have learned that *just* having a negative reaction doesn't ever serve me. It doesn't get me out of the traffic jam, and it doesn't make my kid behave like an angel. So I *choose* gratitude. I choose to change my perception. Think of your negative reaction as a "gift," a reminder to reorient to a new perspective.

Take a look at the optical illusion below.

Some people immediately see two black faces while others see a white vase. Let's say your first reaction is to see the faces. Take a moment to change how you look at it. Can you see the vase? This is what I do in difficult moments: I try to change how I look at it. No matter which image you see at first, they are both there: the vase and the face. You can choose the vase or the face to anchor yourself in the image. In much the same way, I choose to anchor myself through gratitude.

This may sound morbid, but I regularly imagine what my life would be like if I lost all the things I care about. I imagine illness. I imagine my family struggling. I imagine if I lost my belongings, my business, my home. This imagining reminds me how lucky I am. It grounds me in my gratitude deeply and palpably. When I imagine my life without, it makes it very easy to be grateful for what I have. Most of us limit visioning to positive things, but I find it helpful to imagine a variety of futures. One, it prepares you to be resilient for what could come ahead. And two, it helps me be grateful for the comparatively small problems I have right now.

SHARE GRATITUDE

There is always an opportunity to share more gratitude. At the market, make eye contact and thank the person who packed your bags. At work, thank someone for their energy. At home, thank your kids for helping out. If you're a new mama, thank anyone who offers you support. Thank your spouse for running an errand or for simply listening. And then go beyond the words "thank you"—*show* your thanks.

Years ago, I wrote to my first boss to thank him for the opportunity he had given me. I hadn't seen him in well over two decades, but I thanked him for trusting me to run his company and told him how much that experience had had a positive influence on my current business. He called me with tears in his voice and told me that no one had ever thanked him for this. He was filled with such appreciation for my card, and I was filled with such happiness.

There is much research showing that people who practice gratitude have benefits to their health and outlook. Research in the *Journal of Psychotherapy Research* in 2016 showed that the more often you express thanks, the stronger your psychological rewards are for doing it. A study published in 2018 showed that people who wrote letters of gratitude achieved a positive impact on their brain and mental health, even months after they wrote the letter. One of the reasons that this practice works is that you engage in cognitive processing, which helps you focus on the positive aspects of your life. When people participate in positive activities, it increases positive emotions, thoughts, and behaviors.

Don't keep your gratitude to yourself—express it! Take the time to thank the people in your life who have made a positive influence, whether it's a family member, friend, coworker, or even a stranger. Write a heartfelt thank-you note, send a thoughtful text, or simply say, "Thank you," in person. Not only does expressing gratitude strengthen your relationships, but it also reinforces your own sense of appreciation.

SENDING GRATITUDE

A gratitude habit you can build is to send your positive energy. You have surely said before that you are sending someone positive thoughts or healing energy or prayers. But did you know that that energy may work? Everything, including your body, is energy. There have been many studies on what's called "distance healing": this is the idea that energy can be transmitted to another intended person. Results are inconclusive, but it seems that it is possible to send positive healing energy to another. Look at quantum physics: We are all energy, and we all vibrate at different frequencies. The higher vibrations are when we feel love, gratitude, positivity. The lower vibrations are when we feel negativity, stress, depression. The hippies were right: It's all about vibrations. The HeartMath Institute is a nonprofit organization that studies the connection between heart and mind. According to their research, our hearts, brains, and emotions can cause physical vibrations. Positive emotions create a harmonious pattern of heart rate variability, which results in a higher level of coherence in the body's energy field. Activities like smiling, praying, hugging, and expressing gratitude may contribute to a higher vibrational energy field.

COMMUNAL GRATITUDE

Another gratitude habit you can try is a communal gratitude journal. For many years, I had a journal I kept in the kitchen. On most nights when we had dinner as a family, I would ask each person to share one thing they were grateful for, and I recorded it in the journal. I love looking back on what my kids were grateful for at each age.

I have shared the many benefits of gratitude on your health and psychological well-being. When you practice gratitude with others, be it in church or in temple or at your kitchen table, it gives you a shared language and deepens psychosocial connections.

GRATITUDE PRACTICES

Tracking your gratitude practice goals in your Level Up Journal will help you develop them into habits. The following list is by no means complete, but should serve as a guide as you come up with your own practices.

- Write down five things you are grateful for from the previous day.
- Add a note to a gratitude jar each night before dinner.
- Say grace at dinner or share around the table what you are thankful for from the day.
- When you put your kids to bed, each of you share something you are grateful for.

- Think of things you are grateful for when you go to bed.

How this may look in your Level Up Journal:

	MON	TUE	WED	THU	FRI	SAT	SUN
Gratitude journal in the morning (goal: daily)	X		X	X		X	X
Send a Letter to a friend (goal: once a week)		X					

3

GOING SLOWLY

"If you are always racing to the next moment,
what happens to the one you are in?"

– **NANETTE MATHEWS**

In the fast-paced hustle and bustle of modern life, the concept of going slowly might seem counterintuitive, even daunting. Yet buried beneath the relentless pursuit of productivity lies a profound truth: The art of slowing down can be a transformative force, offering a path to deeper fulfillment and enriched experiences.

REDISCOVERING TIME EFFICIENCY

Do you remember the book *Cheaper by the Dozen*? I'm not talking about the movie with Steve Martin. In the movie, the dad was a football coach. But in the book, the dad was a time efficiency expert. I remember a part of the book where he timed how fast he could get the kids out of the house. I can't explain it, but I was lit up by the idea of time efficiency. It's as if it was in my nature to focus on productivity and how to make the most of time.

I have considered myself a productivity expert for a long time now. I have read all of the books on productivity from *Getting Things Done* to *Eat That Frog* to *The Seven Habits of Highly Effective People*. And I became incredibly productive. I could get through a to-do list like nobody's business. But I always felt like I was running on high speed. A million miles an hour. I would make mistakes, and then that would take me more time. I burned out often. I felt like I was never doing a good enough job at work, at parenting, in my marriage, because I was always busy and rushing to the next thing. In the midst of the chaos, I never had time for my own self-care. I knew something needed to change.

I can teach you how to get the most important things done, how to get to inbox zero, and how to maximize your day. Yes, you will be productive. The challenge is that I spent so much time being focused on fast that I missed the gift of going slowly. In our relentless pursuit of ticking off tasks from our to-do lists, we often overlook the profound value of savoring each moment. There is great value in slowing down and not racing through your days.

The allure of speed permeates American culture, manifesting in our obsession with the fastest cars, computers, and smartphones. The prevailing notion is that the individual who accomplishes the most in the shortest span of time emerges victorious. Instant gratification has become the norm, with the convenience of one-click purchases and next-day deliveries shaping our consumer habits; yet, amidst this relentless pace, lies the danger of losing sight of the present moment and sacrificing quality for quantity. We live in a time that reveres hustle.

Do you feel like you are constantly running on a hamster

wheel? Always rushing? That there's never enough time? I get it. I've lived it. And I am telling you that it can be different.

AUDITING LIFE'S PRIORITIES

In the early days of running my business, I was in a constant race between work and motherhood. I left no margin between kid drop-offs and meetings. I finished each day completely wiped out. When I hired my first assistant, she looked at my calendar in total concern. "When do you go to the bathroom? When do you eat?" No wonder I was frazzled. I was double-booked, multitasking, and burning the candle at both ends. I didn't feel like I was doing anything good enough, because everything was frantic and rushed. The realization that incessant rushing breeds chaos can prompt a pivotal question: What aspects of our lives truly merit our time and attention? I had to learn how to audit my priorities, discerning between the essential and the extraneous. The recognition that an overloaded schedule necessitates a reevaluation of life's demands is a crucial step towards reclaiming your time.

By truly evaluating the tasks that consume our days, we gain insight into potential areas for delegation or elimination. Adopting a mindset that prioritizes purpose over busyness empowers us to make deliberate choices about where to invest our energy. The adage, "If it's not a hell yeah, it's a no," serves as a guiding principle, compelling us to align our actions with our deepest values and aspirations.

AN END TO MULTITASKING

If you are multitasking, you are surely trying to go too fast. We multitask because we feel we need to get more done. In my early days as a mom, I thought I was the multitasking queen.

Picture baby Jacob playing on the floor. I would try to work on my computer while my baby was at my feet. I was working, raising babies, cleaning house, prepping meals. And… I was exhausted and not doing anything very well.

In the modern age of constant connectivity, multitasking has become a norm, but recent findings shed light on its detrimental effects on our cognitive health. Research reveals that juggling multiple tasks simultaneously triggers the release of stress hormones like cortisol and adrenaline, leading to brain overstimulation and cognitive impairment. Moreover, multitasking fuels a dopamine addiction loop, rewarding the brain for its scattered focus and perpetual quest for external stimuli.

The irony lies in the fact that the prefrontal cortex, crucial for maintaining focus, is easily swayed by novelty. This innate bias towards novelty hijacks our attention, diverting it towards shiny distractions akin to those captivating infants and pets. Each interruption, be it a phone call, a quick internet search, or checking emails, triggers the brain's reward centers, releasing endogenous opioids and providing momentary pleasure at the expense of sustained focus.

In the past, the lack of constant accessibility meant people could choose when to engage with communication devices; however, the proliferation of mobile phones has created an expectation of constant availability, disrupting traditional boundaries of reachability. This shift is evident in the commonplace sight of individuals interrupting meetings to answer calls, a behavior inconceivable just a few decades ago.

In essence, the allure of multitasking promises quick rewards but ultimately undermines cognitive function, robbing individuals of the profound benefits that stem from sustained focus and undivided attention.

EMBRACING THE GIFT OF STILLNESS

In our fervent quest for productivity, the notion of embracing stillness may initially appear contrary to being productive. However, carving out moments of idleness holds profound benefits for our well-being and creativity. Research indicates that idle time fosters a state of mind conducive to innovation and introspection. When our minds are free to wander, new ideas germinate and creative insights emerge. Your big idea will *never* happen when you are busy.

One of the things you need to make room for in your life is, well, nothing. Sometimes you need to *do nothing*. I don't want you to fill every moment of time. Research shows that when we are idle, our minds wander and we will be more creative. Please note: The impact of idle time on an individual's well-being can vary depending on the context and individual factors. Some research suggests that brief periods of idle time can be beneficial for mental health and creativity, while prolonged periods of idle time can be detrimental to one's physical and mental health. For instance, prolonged periods of idle time, such as long-term unemployment or social isolation, can have negative impacts on an individual's mental and physical health. We saw this on a massive scale during the pandemic. Make note for yourself if a little clear space feels helpful or harmful.

CULTIVATING INTENTIONAL LIVING

Realizing that I hated the feeling of being rushed and always out of time, I had to choose to do less. That is where I started focusing on my MITs for each day. I choose the three most important things to get done. I also block my day to protect my time. For instance, my first thirty minutes and my last thirty minutes at work are blocked out for no appointments. This gives me time to get settled in and to wrap up my day. It prevents chaos if I'm running late to start work (or when my kids were younger, dropping them off to school). I block margin between meetings (so, yes, I can go to the bathroom), and I block time for deep thinking, learning, and quiet time.

By consciously allocating time for rest, reflection, and rejuvenation, we safeguard against the perils of burnout and exhaustion. The pursuit of productivity, while commendable, must not come at the expense of our well-being and fulfillment.

I 100 percent get that the idea of doing less feels overwhelming if you already feel like you aren't getting everything done. When you feel constantly busy and overwhelmed, the inclination is that you must do more. I felt like that. I felt like I couldn't get enough done in a day. I couldn't go fast enough or multitask enough to get through it all. What I needed was a paradigm shift: a realization that I didn't need to do a lot of what I was doing. I needed to do less. I needed to prune.

I once walked outside to find that my gardener had chopped off every last rose on my rose bush. I was devastated. But he explained that you need to prune roses in order to create space and energy for bigger and better blooms. This was a light bulb moment for me. I had lots of roses in my life, but I needed to prune them in order to get space and energy for bigger and better. We need to simplify.

I started to ask myself what could be pruned from my life. Maybe some of these questions will resonate with you.

Do I have to be team mom, room parent, cookie bake sale chef?

Do my kids need to be in multiple sports?

Do I need to drive them back and forth to school, or can I carpool?

Do I need to go to every mom's night out or party or request from a friend?

Do I need to be the one doing all the household chores?

Do I need to do all of the errands, or can I delegate or order home delivery?

What could be done by someone else?

I realized I needed to start saying no to the filler. I started delegating. I started saying no. In order to create a little space to slow down, you will need to do less.

This is hard for everyone, but it is especially hard for the young moms I know. Your time doesn't feel like it's your own. You are constantly juggling children and work and errands and a little bit of self-care if you are very lucky. There is a little bit of, "This is a season of your life" thinking, and that's true. Now that my kids are grown up, I can assure you that the chaos has lessened. But my advice about designing your life around what's most important and starting to delegate will make a big difference.

In the journey towards a slower pace of life, I feel like I have more time, not less. Whether enjoying a leisurely walk with my dogs or relishing a heartfelt conversation with my sister or a friend, the art of slowing down allows me to enjoy each day more fully. In relinquishing the need to constantly rush forward, we open ourselves to the beauty of the present moment, where true abundance awaits.

CONCLUSION

As we navigate the complexities of modern existence, let us heed the wisdom of those who champion the virtues of going slowly. In embracing a deliberate pace, we reclaim ownership of our time and forge a path towards greater fulfillment and meaning. Let us, therefore, embrace the art of slowing down, savoring each moment as a precious gift to be cherished and savored.

In the next chapter, I talk about being present. While it may seem like going slow and being present are the same thing, I see them as different opportunities. Go slowly *and* be present. When you slow down, you have the opportunity to be present.

GOING SLOWLY

Practices to track in your Level Up Journal

As always, this list is just meant to give you ideas for habits you can add to your life.

- Schedule margin (blank space) between meetings, appointments, or activities.
- Start your day with some quiet time.
- End your day with some quiet time.
- Take breaks.
- Put your cell phone away at certain designated times.
- Focus on the person in front of you.
- Put your fork down between bites.
- Hold your cup of coffee with two hands.

How this may look in your Level Up Journal:

	MON	TUE	WED	THU	FRI	SAT	SUN
Create margin on your calendar each day (goal: daily)	X		X	X	X		X
Take a "time out" at the end of each workday	X	X		X	X		

4

BEING PRESENT

"Realize deeply that the present moment is all you ever have. Make the Now the primary focus of your life."

– ECKHART TOLLE

I want you to stand up and walk to the other side of the room. Don't read the next sentence until you do that.

Welcome back. Okay, now I want you to walk to the other side of the room, but be mindful of every step you take. Notice how your foot touches the ground. Notice the change of weight. Don't read the next sentence until you do that.

Welcome back. You are going to walk across the room one more time. But this time, go slowly. Go so slowly, like you are moving through molasses. Pause for a moment before putting your foot down. What is the slowest you can move without being still?

Now you feel what it is to be mindful. And to go slowly.

As I said, I was tempted to include this topic in the previous chapter about going slowly. But being present and going slowly are not the same thing. Going slowly implies a deliberate pace or rhythm in how you approach things. It's about intentionally slowing down your actions, thoughts, or the pace of life in general. Going slowly can help you savor each moment, deepen your understanding, and reduce stress by avoiding rushing through tasks or experiences. On the other hand, being present typically involves focusing your attention on the current moment, fully engaging with whatever is happening right now without judgment or distraction. It's about immersing yourself in the present experience, whether it's a conversation, a task, or simply being aware of your surroundings. Being present allows you to fully appreciate and experience life as it unfolds, rather than dwelling on the past or worrying about the future.

Every report card I ever got said that I was a daydreamer—and it was not a compliment. As a kid with ADD, I for sure had no control of my monkey brain. It was very difficult for me to focus. That's one of the reasons school was such a challenge for me. It was pretty hard to read a chapter, much less a book, if your mind was traveling somewhere else. I spent a good part of my life growing up feeling poorly about my past and worrying about my future. Sound familiar to your own life? What happens to the present moment if we are never living there?

Jason (my husband) said if he could change just one thing about me, it would be my absentmindedness. I'm telling you: It's a real thing for me. Don't believe me? Listen to these stories.

My dad planned an amazing sixtieth birthday cruise with our entire family. We were all so excited. When we got to the cruise check-in, they asked for my son's birth certificate. I had no idea that you needed a birth certificate when bringing a child on a cruise. Not only did we not have it with us, we did not have it at all. We couldn't get on the cruise. My dad and my four-year-old son hugged and sobbed as we had to depart. It was one of the most heartbreaking moments of my life. We had to drive home and leave the rest of my family on the cruise. This was Saturday, and the county services office, where we needed to get the birth certificate, didn't open until Monday. We had to fly out later to catch up with my family, missing days of the cruise.

Here's another one. I bought tickets to take the family to a Padres game (our baseball team). We got dressed up in our gear and pulled up in the parking lot, only to find it strangely empty. We start walking towards the stadium, and Jason said, "Babe, something is off. This place should be packed. Can you check the tickets?" I did. They were playing; but not in San Diego. I had bought tickets to a game in another city.

I've got one more for you. I had first row tickets for the family to see Disney on Ice… in Spanish. I should have known when Mickey came out saying, "Hola." My kids wanted to leave, but I told them that ice-skating was a universal language.

Forget about joy. My monkey brain was causing me pain, and the only remedy was to practice presence.

MEDITATION

> "Buddha was asked, 'What have you gained from meditation?' He replied, 'Nothing. However, let me tell you what I've lost. I have lost anger, anxiety, depression, insecurity, fear of old age, and death.'"

The first and most powerful way that I have learned presence is through meditation. I have been meditating for over thirty years. Never ever has there been a session where I sat with no thoughts. Why? Because it's not possible. The mind thinks and moves. That's what it does. I meditate to slow my thoughts down. To let them settle. To create a little space between the thoughts.

Let me tell you how I got started. I took yoga classes from a friend and mentor, Michele Hebert. I'm not sure if she will even remember this story that I'm about to tell you. I was her guest at a beautiful resort called Rancho La Puerta. I accidentally messed up giving her directions to my house, and she arrived very stressed out after getting caught in traffic and getting all turned around. This was before GPS. Heck, this was before cell phones. I had actually never seen my calm, spiritual friend so flustered. I guess she was human.

As soon as we arrived at The Ranch, she took me to a special meditation room so she could decompress and regain her spirit. We took a seated meditation pose. And we sat. And sat. And sat. It was *so* painful for me. There was nothing relaxing about it. *How long is she going to sit like that? How long are we going to be here? How long have we been here? My hips are killing me. Can I move?* I thought. Needless to say, it was not relaxing for me—at all! When I expressed my discontent to Michele, she explained that it's a practice, and that means you have to practice. Maybe you start with one minute, then two, and so on.

If this whole thing is so hard, why would we want to do it? I'll tell you why. Science studying neuroplasticity of the brain has shown the concrete and indisputable benefits of meditation.

Your Reticular Activating System has you focus on only what you tell it to be aware of. For instance, think about your right arm right now. I bet you weren't thinking of it before! But now you are aware of it. Your brain will focus on what you tell it to. Meditation and a regular mindfulness practice has been proven to physically rebuild our brains—and thus improve our lives. It is actually the act of bringing your mind back to your focus that strengthens it.

The following are all scientifically proven benefits to meditation:

- It increases your immune system.
- It decreases stress.
- It improves your memory, attention, and focus. Basically, it is strengthening your brain.
- It's good for your body in ways we don't totally understand. It has positive effects on heart disease, osteoporosis, sleep problems, digestive problems, depression, and obesity.
- It's even good for our relationships. Couples say that they become more loving when they meditate. No, I have not gotten Jason to meditate. I'm just saying that the science shows it's good stuff.

Don't make too much of how to meditate. It's really as simple as sitting quietly. The goal is not to have no thoughts. That will basically never happen. A mind never turns off. But the chatter does quiet, with practice. You can focus on your breath, or a word, or a mantra. You can focus on a sound. Over the last few years, I have been doing a lot of breathwork practice. This is also a form of meditation and tends to be easier for many than just sitting in lotus position doing a typical meditation.

I absolutely swear to you that my days go better on the days that I meditate. I feel more grounded, calmer. Maybe I don't notice that as much as I notice that on the days that I don't meditate, I am more agitated, quicker to yell... definitely more stressed. I respond better to the chaos of family life when I meditate in the morning.

My morning practice looks something like this: I wake up before the family does. I take about ten minutes to journal and then read a passage or quote from an inspirational book. I then set a time for eleven minutes (eleven only because it's my favorite number) and sit. I also put on some soft nature music or meditation music that I find on iTunes or Spotify. Sometimes I do a guided meditation. Sometimes I practice mantra meditation.

That's it. What has happened after practicing for so long is that my mind goes into that relaxed space quite quickly. Some days, it doesn't, and that's okay. Some days, I feel I need to meditate again. If I'm feeling particularly stressed or anxious, I tell the kids that Mommy needs a time-out, and I'll go meditate. Funnily enough, what has happened is that my daughter Rachel has gotten curious and has joined me. Actually, both kids have joined me before. When they were little, they liked one meditation that I do where I sit in front of a candle and try to still the flame by being very quiet on the outside and the inside. Rachel loved this rainbow breath meditation that I do.

It goes something like this:

RAINBOW BREATH

Get comfortable.
Stretch if you need to.
Maybe put your hands on your belly or by your side.
Close your eyes.
Gaze inward.
Take a deep beautiful breath.
Breathe in.
Breathe out.

Purposefully bring your breath up through your spine.
Purposefully move your breath down your spine.
Breathe out. Down your spine.
Breathe in. Up your spine.
Breathe down to the base of your spine.
Light the base a beautiful deep red.
Feel the color red.
Feel its heat.
Its vibrance.
Feel the color red.
Red is the color of love, energy, and strength.
Breathe in.
Breathe out.
Send the breath to your pelvis. Make it the color orange.
Light the color a bright orange.
Feel the color orange.
Feel its radiance.
Orange is the color of courage, confidence, success.

Send the breath to your belly.
Light the color a beautiful yellow.
Feel the color yellow.
Feel its warmth.
Its energy.
Feel the color yellow.
Yellow is the color of energy, intellect, happiness.

Breathe in.
Breathe out.

Send your breath to your heart. Make it the color green.
Feel the color green.
Feel its life.
Its energy.
Green is the color of love, hope, compassion.
Feel the color green.

Send your breath to throat. Make the breath turquoise.
Feel the color turquoise.
Feel its healing.
Its energy.
Turquoise is the color of communication. Of creativity. Of your spirituality.
Breathe in.
Breathe out.

Send your breath to your imaginary third eye. Make the breath blue.
Feel the color blue.
Feel its tranquility.
Its energy.
Blue is the color of trust, intuition, loyalty.
Breathe in.
Breathe out.

Finally, send the breath to the top of your head. To your crown. Make this color lavender.
Feel the color lavender.
Its energy.
Lavender is the color of enlightenment and understanding.
Breathe in.

Breathe out.
Breathe a long breath and light all of the colors of the rainbow.
Red
Orange
Yellow
Green
Turquoise
Blue
Lavender

Let your breath just flow.
Do what it wants to do.
Seal this meditation with a breath of love.

Please go to www.levelupyourlifebook.com for access to free meditations.

MINDFULNESS

Have you ever cleared through a box of cookies while watching TV, only to look down and realize you don't even remember eating them? Or you got to work and don't even remember the drive? These would be examples of a lack of mindfulness. We are going through life on autopilot, which is partly why most of us have lost the joy of living. We are simply missing it.

"Mindfulness" is quite the buzz word nowadays. Really, it's pretty simple in concept. Your mind is attending to whatever you are presently doing. This is simple but not easy in today's day and age because of the multitude of distractions we have. From pings of texts, emails, pop-ups… it is difficult to be present.

Mindfulness is really just being present in the moment. It's paying attention to whatever you are doing. And the benefits are astounding. You will feel lower stress and anxiety, better sleep, increased happiness, and, yes, more joy. What I love about mindfulness is that it's already within you and you can practice it at any time. Think of any activity that you do on autopilot. All of those are activities where you can practice mindfulness. It doesn't matter if you are driving, walking, or doing the dishes; you can be present in the moment. The activity is the anchor. You want to focus on your breath and whatever you are doing. Your mind will wander, so don't you dare judge yourself when it does. Use that mind wandering as a reminder to come back to the activity at hand.

The funny thing is you can even be mindful with your wandering mind. Just give yourself some space to pay attention to your jumbled thoughts. Watch them with curiosity. *Oh, isn't that interesting that that's what I'm thinking about?* You watching your thoughts on purpose is you being mindful.

You aren't going to practice this all day long. But it's great to come to it throughout the day. Just connect to the moment. Again, you are training your brain like a muscle. The more you do it, the stronger it will get. The easier it will be.

Practice mindfulness in the nooks and crannies of your day. It's great to practice at times that feel stressful. For example, sitting in traffic is a great time to be present. Connect to your breath. Follow it in and out. Feel your body relax. Let go.

DIGITAL DETOX

This is a topic that has been the most difficult for me to master. It's still a work in progress. I'm talking about my connection to my devices—or disconnection, for that matter). What I know is that I want to live a more present and fulfilling life, and that it is blocked by this little computer screen that lives in my hand.

So, I have been working at creating a digital philosophy for myself to help me find a more balanced healthy relationship with screen time.

Did you know that:

- 85 percent of Americans use their phone while talking to others?
- 80 percent check it within an hour of getting up and before going to bed?
- 47 percent have tried to limit their phone usage, but only 30 percent have been successful?

We are the "looking down" generation. Look around, my friends. At parks, at appointments, at restaurants, even in cars. Everyone is looking down at their phones. We are missing out on life. It's not our fault; they are designing for our weakness. Software designers get paid big bucks to keep you addicted to your screen.

It's not just about wasting your time. It's actually bad for our health. Your screen time might affect:

- Vision
- Sleep
- Addiction / Reward Seeking
- Weight
- Overall Health
- Learning
- Social Skills

Think you aren't addicted?
Is your phone the first thing you reach for in the morning?

Is it the last thing ?
Do you check your phone more than twenty times per day?
Are you sure?
Do you bring your phone to the dinner table?
Do you check your phone while you're driving?
At a light?
Be honest.

I've got a new word for you: nomophobia. This is the fear of being without your phone. You *freak* out if you can't find your phone in your pockets. Literally, you would turn the whole house upside down just to find your phone.

Do you feel the need to reach for your phone every time you stop at a traffic light? Do you stress out when you don't have a connection and can't read your feed?

On average, it's estimated that people in the U.S. check their phones around **96 times per day**, or roughly once every 10 minutes while awake. This number has been steadily increasing over the years, reflecting the growing dependence on mobile devices for communication, information, and entertainment.

What are we checking most often? Social media.

At the time of writing this book..

The average user spends thirty-five minutes on Facebook per day.

An average Instagram user surfs for fifteen minutes a day.

The average user spends twenty-five minutes a day on Snapchat.

There's not a whole lot that I remember from my psychology classes, but I do remember the power of intermittent reinforcement. This means that the reinforcement (or reward) is given only sometimes. Because we sometimes get a reward for picking it up, we keep picking it up. Every time you check, dopamine jackpot! You get a hit of something that feels good.

The problem (well, there are many problems with this) is that we are living in fight or flight mode. Back in the caveman days, you would go into fight or flight when you encountered a sabertooth tiger. I'm not sure why that is always the caveman example but let's go with it. That was a super helpful response. And luckily that didn't happen very often, so most of the time you could just chill out, pick some berries, and connect over the fire. But your brain has not evolved. Every time you get a ping from your device, it puts you in fight or flight mode. And the problem is that we have very little time to sit and pick berries so to speak. We are always on. It is wearing on your brain and your physiology.

This whole thing started as a novelty. It was fun. I remember being so excited about being able to listen to my favorite music on my iPod, or being able to connect with an old friend from high school on social media.

We used to log on to log off from life.

But now we need to log off to log into life.

These devices are not going away. I'm afraid they will one day be implanted in us. Everything in moderation right?

We need to create a philosophy for our digital health.

What do you want to do with your life?

What's most important to you?

I'm pretty sure that your life is happening while you're looking down at your cell phone.

This might sound crazy, but we need to take a cue from the Amish. I'm guessing you assume that the Amish don't use any technology, but that's not actually true. They test out technology and see if the technology adds value to their life, if it is in line with their values. If it's not, they decide not to use it. Look at what you use each day. What is adding value? There definitely are good things. I love my Audible account, my podcasts, my meditation apps, and my workout tracking apps. Just be honest with yourself if you are spending your time on things that charge you up.

Here are five steps you can take to digital detox your life:

1. Turn off notifications on your phone and computer
2. Create a physical boundary from your device. Put your phone in an "unplugged" box at home. Put your phone in a purse or glove compartment in your car.
3. Set time limits on screen time and on apps that you use.
4. Unsubscribe and delete apps that don't benefit your life.
5. Pick one day a week to take a sabbatical from your phone.

Think about that charge light on your cell phone. When you see it running low, you will search high and low for a cord and an outlet to make sure you don't run out of battery. How about your own light? What are you doing to make sure that you personally stay charged?

BE HERE NOW

When my kids were little, I remember rushing them to naps or wishing they would hurry up when putting their shoes on. I was always rushing. Trying to get back to work. Trying to get more done. Looking back, I wish I hadn't rushed it all. I wish I didn't say, "Hurry up!" as often as I did. Our kids have gifts to share about being present. They will stare in wonder at a bug in the street. They revel in playing in puddles and swinging on the swingset. They are not caught up in their thoughts, riddled with worry or stress or anxiety.

I plan a lot of vacations. In the past, I would spend so much time planning and thinking about the vacation, but when I got there, it was hard to stop thinking about work. When I did stop, I thought about how I didn't want the vacation to end. Then I thought about what vacation I would plan next. I missed the very experience I had worked so hard for. Now, I let it go. I let work go. I immerse myself in the experience. And I don't plan the next one until I get home.

We spend so much of our day worrying about the future and stressing about the past. We miss the present moment. Our thoughts rule our day; but you are not your thoughts. You can observe your thoughts, but your truth is in what you are doing right now. Be in this moment. Appreciate the sunset. Savor the cookie. Feel the warmth of the hug.

> When you are at work: Work.
> When you are with your kids: Be with them.
> When you are with you: Soak it up.

BEING PRESENT HABITS

Here are some practices to track in your Level Up Journal. As always, this list is just meant to give you ideas for habits you can add to your life.

- Meditate
- Breathwork exercises
- Turn off notifications
- Take social media off your phone
- Unitask (instead of multitasking)
- Eat without having a device or TV on

How this may look in your Level Up Journal:

	MON	TUE	WED	THU	FRI	SAT	SUN
Meditate for ten minutes every morning (goal: daily)			X			X	X
Put phone away at 7:00 p.m. (goal: daily)	X		X	X			X

LIVE WITH YOUR SENSES

"To live to your fullest, live with all of your five senses."

– ME, LISA DRUXMAN

When you were a child you learned about your five senses: sight, smell, sound, taste, and touch. Each one of them is really important in your everyday life. You use at least one of your five senses every moment of every day. Your senses work together to let your brain know what is going on around you. They help to keep you safe by warning you of any danger. Yet we hardly pay meaningful attention to our senses. I have found that tapping into these senses creates a deeper sense of living. I want to share with you how I am using my senses to create joy in my daily living.

SMELL
Let's start with smell. Ah, the smell of freshly baked cookies. Or the smell of a baby's skin. Our sense of smell is a powerful conduit to our memories, capable of transporting us back in time with just a whiff of a familiar scent. Whether it's the

comforting embrace of a loved one's perfume or the crisp scent of autumn leaves, each fragrance holds within it a world of emotions waiting to be unlocked. The sense of smell might be the strongest sense to bring back a feeling or take you back to a special moment. There is a soap that, if I smell it, I remember taking the best bubble bath I've ever had, while on my ten-year anniversary in Paris. It was one of the happiest times of my life, and I can bring back that memory instantly with a simple scent. It unfortunately is not a time machine, so of course I'm not actually back there, but bringing back those memories is joyful. A scent travels through your brain and can trigger feel-good endorphins and serotonin.

Here is how I tap into the sense of smell in my day. When I meditate in the morning, I either light incense or burn sage. I have such a strong connection to these scents with my meditation practice that the smell of them alone helps me connect to my desired state of being. Incense has been used for thousands of years in many ceremonies. There have been studies that show that incense can calm and boost mood due to a compound within it. Find an aroma that appeals to you. Burning sage—also known as smudging—is an ancient spiritual ritual. The most-used types of sage have antimicrobial properties. I will not get into the spiritual aspect of smudging and will stick with the properties of smell. Similar to incense, it seems that the smell of certain plants can create a reaction in the brain that may increase peace or happiness.

Each day, I use aromatherapy oils in my routine to tap into my sense of scent. I use a diffuser in my home office. Citrus smells help me feel happy. Minty oils help me feel alert. Frankincense helps me feel grounded and meditative. At the end of every day, I rub on lavender oil as part of my nighttime routine to help me get settled and sleepy. I don't sell oils, and I'm not an oil expert. (I'm sure all of the oil reps will gladly make comments on this chapter with their recommendations.) I just know that the various smells make me feel good. Beyond aromatherapy oils, I regularly use good-smelling candles and incense to set my mood.

TASTE

Engaging fully with your sense of taste can be a doorway to living more fully. Taste is not just about satisfying hunger or enjoying flavors; it's a multi-dimensional experience that can connect you with the present moment, enhance your appreciation for food, and even improve your overall well-being. Think of the taste of your favorite food, and I bet you will find the joy. For me, this comes mainly in the form of being present while I eat. No TV, no devices, no phone. When I created LEAN (a behavior modification weight management program), I did an activity called "sensperience." I would blindfold you or have you close your eyes and then have you taste different foods.

The Sensperience is used to enhance your senses in regard to hunger and food. I want you to enjoy food with all your senses: the aroma, the taste, the texture. Eat beautiful foods with a colorful palette. In order to eat with your senses, you need to take time. So in regards to your taste, notice the temperature, the texture. Is it sweet or salty? Experience your food fully. There may be science to why the taste of chocolate makes you happy. Interestingly enough, spicy foods and tumeric may also increase happiness.

Several studies have explored the benefits of mindful eating practices. For example, research published in the journal *Appetite* found that participants who engaged in mindful eating techniques reported increased enjoyment of food and decreased consumption of unhealthy snacks compared to those who ate mindlessly. Another study in the *Journal of Obesity* demonstrated that mindfulness-based interventions for eating behaviors led to significant reductions in binge eating and emotional eating among participants.

Incorporating mindfulness into your relationship with food doesn't require any special equipment or training; it simply involves being present and attentive while you eat. Start by taking a few deep breaths before your meal to center yourself and bring your awareness to the present moment. As you eat, pay attention to the flavors, textures, and sensations of each bite and try to eat slowly and mindfully. With practice, you may find that being present to your sense of taste not only enhances your enjoyment of food but also enriches your overall experience of life.

SIGHT

Our eyes are the windows to the soul, offering glimpses into the beauty that surrounds us. From the vibrant hues of a sunset to the intricate patterns of a snowflake, the world is brimming with visual wonders waiting to be discovered. By curating our living spaces with meaningful objects and colors that resonate with our spirit, we can transform our surroundings into sanctuaries of joy and inspiration.

Numerous studies have explored the impact of visual aesthetics on our mood and mental well-being. Research published in the *Journal of Environmental Psychology* found that exposure to natural elements, such as plants and sunlight, can significantly reduce stress and anxiety levels, while enhancing feelings of happiness and vitality. By incorporating elements of nature into our indoor environments, such as potted plants and natural light sources, we can create a more harmonious and uplifting space that nurtures both body and soul.

In addition to natural elements, the arrangement and organization of our surroundings can also influence our emotional state. A study conducted by researchers at the University of California, Los Angeles, found that cluttered environments can lead to feelings of overwhelm and anxiety, while clean and organized spaces promote a sense of calm and clarity. By decluttering our living spaces and surrounding ourselves with meaningful objects that bring us joy, we can create a visual landscape that reflects our innermost desires and aspirations.

Furthermore, the colors we choose to adorn our surroundings can have a profound impact on our mood and emotional well-being. Research in the field of color psychology has shown that different colors evoke specific emotional responses in individuals. For example, warm colors such as red and orange are associated with feelings of energy and passion, while cool colors such as blue and green are linked to calmness and tranquility. By selecting colors that resonate with our personal preferences and goals, we can create a visual environment that uplifts and inspires us on a daily basis.

If I look around my home and see dirt or clutter, it does not feel good. When I look around and see meaningful items such as pictures of my kids or mementos from vacations, it brings me joy. When I see a clutter-free desk or an organized drawer, it brings me joy. You do not have to have a Pinterest- or Instagram-curated home to find joy in your surroundings. Choose colors that make you feel good. Open up the blinds. Light impacts how you feel. Jason and I have argued for years about opening our shutters in our room. He hates to think of someone looking in, which I get. But I hate having a dark room. Closed shutters are almost symbolic of sadness or being closed off to the day. When I explained it like that, he opens them up every day... after we get dressed, of course. As I look around my office right now, I feel joy. I am surrounded with quotes and pictures and candles and even some crystals. They are joyful images for me. What might bring you joy?

TOUCH

Touch is the first sense. It's the one most developed in babies, so it's natural that touch is very important. We have all heard about that babies need to be cuddled to develop properly. If touch weren't important, we wouldn't have bumper stickers that say, "Did you hug your child today?"

Did you know that touch is the only sense that doesn't diminish with age? The sense of touch is an important one in bringing joy.

Nerve endings in the skin and in other parts of the body send information to the brain. There are four kinds of touch sensations that can be identified: cold, heat, contact, and pain. I do not get joy from cold or pain. But I do love the feel of a warm fire or even my heater under my desk on a chilly day. The sense of touch could be the softness of a T-shirt. I have a pair of soft cabin socks that bring me joy every time I put them on. But for daily joy, it's my favorite fuzzy blanket that I snuggle with every single night.

I think the most important sense of touch is human contact. The first thing I think of when I think of skin to skin contact is sex. I once heard a therapist say that if you wait until both of you are in the mood, you'll never have sex. Be purposeful and have it regularly. Not only is sex a form of exercise, it also reduces pain, improves sleep, boosts self-esteem, lowers menstrual pain, lowers blood pressure… the list goes on.

It doesn't even have to be that intimate. Deep hugs. Skin on skin. Holding hands. Think about how good it feels to have your hair washed when you get it cut. Think about how good it feels to get your feet rubbed when you get a pedicure. I set a goal for myself to get a massage regularly. That touch is life-giving to me!

The act of touch has been shown to release oxytocin, often referred to as the "love hormone," which plays a key role in bonding and social connection. A study published in the journal *Psychological Science* found that participants who engaged in supportive touch, such as holding hands or giving hugs, experienced increased levels of oxytocin and greater feelings of trust and intimacy towards their partners. By incorporating touch into our daily interactions and relationships, we can strengthen our connections with others and cultivate a deeper sense of belonging and affection.

A little side note about touch: It's actually a good thing to be touchy-feely. Studies of professional sports teams showed the teams that had the most high fives, most hugs, and the most fist bumps performed better!

SOUND

Finally, let's talk about the sense of sound in finding the joy of living. We obviously depend on our hearing a lot. To communicate, to hear notices from phones, doorbells, the honk of a horn. But you can also use sound to create joy. I mean it makes sense: If hearing the shriek of an alarm or the cry of a baby makes you feel unsettled, then clearly other sounds can bring peace or happiness.

Let's start with music. Music is incredibly powerful. It can evoke emotions. What song makes you happy? What song pumps you up? What if you created a soundtrack to play while on a run, at work, or in the car? How about choosing a favorite song to wake you up? It might sound silly (no pun intended). But I often put on classical music when I'm cooking. Getting dinner cooked after getting home from work and while the kids are doing homework is not typically my favorite time of day. It often feels rushed and chaotic. So I create my atmosphere. I light a candle or two (this affects both my sight and my smell), and I put on some soothing music. The kids make fun of me, but I don't care. It is an anchor for me to chill out.

If you live or work somewhere with lots of noise, you might want to create the absence of sound. Get some good noise-cancelling headphones so you can find peace when you want it.

I have recently been introduced to a new way to use sound. It's called sound bathing. This is where you immerse yourself in listening to a variety of frequencies and is an ancient practice that is becoming popular in many yoga type of classes. Tibetans have been using it for over two thousand years. They use singing bowls, chimes, gongs, and various percussion to create vibrations. Sound baths are meant to help create a shift in your brainwave state. With sound it is possible to shift from our normal beta state (your normal waking state) to an alpha state (which is relaxed consciousness). In sound bathing, many people are able to reach theta (meditative) state and even delta state (where internal healing can occur). It's nothing I can really describe. I have this incredible feeling that passes through my body from the sounds. It's actually a physical release. I am in awe of the experience of it, so it's something that I am now researching more fully. I have my own singing bowl and chime that I use as part of my morning meditation practice. You can find some digital versions on YouTube and in some meditation apps. But, really, to feel the vibrations, try the real thing.

I'm sure that sound bathing isn't for everyone. Just try some different ways to tap into the sense of sound to bring you more joy. Listen to your child's laughter. Sing a song. Listen to your breath. Listen to the sound of the wind in the trees or to the sound of running water.

So those are the five senses; but you already knew those. It's about bringing about an awareness of them, truly living with all of your senses. I believe that this is helping me live more deeply and not just on the surface of my day.

LIVING WITH YOUR SENSES

Here are some practices to track in your Level Up Journal. As always, this list is just meant to give you ideas for habits you can add to your life.

- Use aromatherapy oils (Smell)
- Play soothing music (Hearing)
- Make your screen saver a beautiful painting (Sight)
- Appreciate the taste of your foods without distraction (Taste)
- Massage your feet at the end of the day (Touch)

How this may look in your Level Up Journal:

	MON	TUE	WED	THU	FRI	SAT	SUN
Play classical music while working	X	X		X	X		
Burn sage in the morning	X	X	X		X		X

YOUR VILLAGE

> "The beauty of a village lies not only in its landscapes but in the love and support of its people."
>
> **– UNKNOWN**

FIT4MOM is the largest fitness program for moms in the United States and has been for the last two decades. We have probably touched the lives of a million moms. The *number one* reason that my company has seen such amazing success is the connections created in our classes. Moms come for the fitness, but they stay for the community. When moms come to FIT4MOM, they realize they aren't alone; they bond over their shared experiences. They get support. They laugh. They lean on one another. All human beings have a need to connect, to belong. We are a biologically social species, but in the age of social media and smart phones, it has become increasingly difficult to build real relationships. It's as if we've forgotten how to connect.

According to anthropologist Robin Dunbar, early hunter-gatherer societies would have roughly 150 connections.

According to his theory, people would have five loved ones, fifteen good friends, fifty friends, and 150 meaningful connections. Our ancestors benefitted from being in a tribe; being around others signaled safety. Changes in family structure and the spread of digital communities have led to fewer meaningful connections. We tend to live alone with our immediate family, instead of extended family. We tend to have a handful friends whom we see on occasion. We may have thousands of "friends" on social media, but we have lost true connection. When we are isolated, we activate a biological defense mechanism, which can cause higher blood pressure, anxiety, stress hormones, and an inflammatory response. These days, we are so very isolated. We don't support each other as we did in the time of our ancestors. We are very alone.

In today's day and age of busy, our relationships are suffering. Relationships, whether with parents, children, a spouse, or friends, need tending to just like a garden. They need nourishment and time.

If labeled, I am an introvert. Most people think of an introvert as someone who is shy and quiet. It's more about energy. Extroverts are energized by being with lots of people. Introverts are energized from time with self. I am a CEO and public speaker, so clearly I know how to socialize and can network with the best of them. It just doesn't give me energy. The easy path for me is to be by myself. I like my own company (no, I'm not talking about FIT4MOM). I get along very well with myself. There are no communication issues with just me. There is no conflict. But I also know that being alone does not help me live my best life. The wider and deeper my social connections, the more fully I live.

To be honest, I didn't start Stroller Strides to have a business.

I started it because I needed community, and I was too uncomfortable to join a mom's group. I started a program where all moms would be welcomed. It didn't matter your fitness level, your skin color, your size. It didn't matter if you breast-fed or bottle-fed. We would welcome you, and we still do. I thought Stroller Strides was solving a fitness void. But in reality, we are solving for a community void.

The ritual of women gathering to connect and share stories is universal and as old as humankind in virtually every culture. For thousands of years women gathered in nature, around campfires or sacred spaces to share resources, pass down wisdom, traditions, medicine, and lessons. The more they shared and connected, the more powerful they became together. When women had babies, the entire village took care of both the mom and baby. In some cultures today this still exists.

Unfortunately this began to change as we moved to a nuclear family society, both parents secluded in a home. Women's circles, rituals, and community decreased. We were isolated and expected to do everything on our own. This new structure created something known as a "sister wound." The sister wound lives in all of us. It is the silent voice that tells us we don't belong with others.

> I'm too much.
> I'm too anxious.
> I'm too busy.
> They won't like me.
> I don't have anything to give.

The sister wound convinces you that you won't fit in with a new group of women. It is the reason we automatically make comparisons between ourselves and others. It's the voice that tells us we aren't good enough or we'll never be as successful or as beautiful as another woman is.

But if we tap into our true nature, we realize that as humans we are made to connect and that group healing is part of our nature.

That's why community is so important. Through connection, we emerge empowered and supported, knowing we are never alone and that, together, anything is possible. When people are part of a community they have better health (both physically and mentally), increased confidence, self-esteem, emotional connection, and so much more. Community is instrumental in encouraging people to be their best selves and recognize that we are more powerful when we come together.

ALONE WITH OUR PHONE

Yes, I know we have already talked about devices in the Digital Detox section, but it's impossible not to address the biggest obstacle to our real-life connections. I am the last generation to remember what it was like not to have a smart phone. I remember the day that Jason and I got our first iPhones. We went on a date, went to the Apple Store, and then went to a cozy and quiet little local bar with our new devices. We opened them up and spent the next few hours in total immersion, lost in our new devices. That began the end of being disconnected.

In an era where our smartphones have become extensions of ourselves, it's paradoxical how these devices, designed to connect us, often leave us feeling more alone than ever before. With a swipe and a tap we enter a digital realm where the world is at our fingertips, yet actually human touch feels distant, replaced by screens and algorithms.

Our phones have become our constant companions, always

within arm's reach, ready to distract us from the silence of our own thoughts. We find solace in the glow of their screens, seeking validation in likes and comments, but the connection they offer is often superficial, leaving us craving something deeper.

Social media, once hailed as a tool for bringing people together, has inadvertently become a breeding ground for loneliness. We scroll through curated feeds, comparing our lives to carefully crafted highlight reels, and in the process we lose sight of genuine connection. Instead of fostering meaningful relationships, we find ourselves trapped in a cycle of envy and insecurity, longing for the illusion of perfection.

Even in the presence of others, our phones can act as barriers, shielding us from the discomfort of face-to-face interaction. We bury ourselves in virtual worlds, retreating into the safety of our screens rather than engaging with the world around us. Conversation becomes stilted and eye contact fleeting as we prioritize the digital over the tangible.

But perhaps the most insidious aspect of smartphone-induced isolation is its subtle erosion of our ability to be alone. Constant connectivity means we're never truly by ourselves, always reachable at the touch of a button. Yet in our perpetual quest for connection, we overlook the value of solitude, of quiet moments spent in self-reflection and introspection.

The irony is that in our pursuit of connection, we've never been more disconnected from ourselves and each other. Our phones, once heralded as harbingers of a more connected world, have become symbols of our collective loneliness.

I know that this feels very doom and gloom. There are of course many positive things that come from these devices; but I think we need to be purposeful about how we use them in our lives. Amidst the sea of screens, there remains hope for genuine connection, if only we can muster the courage to look up, to reach out, and to embrace the messy, imperfect beauty of human interaction. I am very purposeful to create plans with real people on a regular basis. I have monthly dates with friends for game nights, hikes, breakfasts, and walks. I am purposeful about who I surround myself with.

THE FIVE PEOPLE YOU SURROUND YOURSELF WITH

Jim Rohn once said, "You are the average of the five people you spend the most time with." For the past two decades, I have been very purposeful about my circle. I seek out friends who lift me up, who inspire me, who make me laugh, who make me want to be a better person. I have put space between friends who are a constant source of energy drain, complaining, victimhood, and negativity.

I have stretched myself out of my comfort zone to join new networks. I have joined entrepreneur and CEO groups such as Vistage, Michael Hyatt's Business Accelerator, EO, and Strategic Coach. This puts me in a community of high-achieving, successful people.

I will share with you what's working for me. Deepening these connections is bringing more joy to my daily life. Each one of these is a work in progress. I am imperfect but at least aim towards doing better. In this chapter, I share how I am purposeful in building relationships with my spouse, family, and friends.

One of the biggest areas of regret for people is loss of connections. We lose contact with friends and family because we are too busy. If you can connect with that regret, then it's time to reconnect with people. Reach out to friends and family. Make it a point to nurture the relationships in your life.

RELATIONSHIPS

There is an activity that we do at our FIT4MOM events, called the Eye Contact Experiment. You take two people and have them look deep into each other's eyes. No words. No facial gestures. Just look into each other's eyes. First, you will notice how uncomfortable it is. What ends up happening for most people is an intense feeling of emotion. You will regularly see people (even if they are complete strangers) start to cry when they look into each other's eyes. Try it. You will be amazed. The first time I did this experiment was standing next to a man I had never met. Within a few minutes, tears started to stream down his face. Then mine started. When we debriefed after, he said that he cried because he realized he had not looked into his wife's eyes since they had gotten married. He couldn't wait to get home to connect with her.

What are the foundations of a loving relationship for you? What is essential? Think about it for a moment before you read on.

Honesty?

Trust?

Kindness?

Passion?

Loyalty?

Respect?

Acceptance?

Encouraging?

Now, before you start measuring if you are getting them from your spouse or another relationship, I want to ask you a question.

Are you giving those things to yourself?

Are you being kind to yourself? Accepting? Encouraging? Fill in the blanks with your own words.

I truly believe that before you can build relationships with others, you need to build a relationship with yourself. You cannot expect these things from others if you can't give them to yourself.

You hear that tiny voice that is constantly talking to you, even while you are doing other activities in the day. That little voice is even talking to you while you are reading this book. Is it kind? Is it helpful? Is it judging or belittling? Our brains are programmed to be negative, so don't be surprised to find that the little voice isn't rooting you on. You have probably heard this before, but I will share again as it's pretty powerful: You think approximately 60,000 thoughts per day. Ninety-eight percent of those thoughts are the same thoughts you had from the previous day. If your thoughts are wired to be negative, just imagine what you are feeding your brain. If you feed your body bad stuff, what do you think will happen? Likewise, if you feed your mind bad stuff, what do you think will happen?

No matter how long it has been talking to you this way, it can be changed. Remember when we talked about neuroplasticity (the ability for the brain to change)? There are a variety of techniques to start retraining the brain. Think of it like potty training a puppy: When it makes a mess, you just keep bringing it back to the spot you want it to go. There's no reason for anger. Just bring it back. When you have a thought that doesn't serve you, first just be aware of it. *Oh, that's interesting that that came up for me. Well, that thought doesn't serve me.* You don't have to beat yourself up or judge yourself for going there. Just notice it. The next step is to do a do-over thought, which we talked about in the section on gratitude. Be kind to yourself. See what happens when you feed your brain with support and love like you want in a loving relationship.

Beyond the words, what are some self-love habits you might

practice? Are there things you can do each day that make you feel good? Make you happy? Help you feel joy? I think you will find that the practices in this book, from meditation to gratitude, will be the foundation to having a good relationship with yourself.

Being in a good state with things like meditation is easy when you are by yourself. The hard part is being in a good state when you are with others. I kind of get why Buddhist monks can be so peaceful. They live a solitary life and are only with people who have the same thoughts and beliefs. This is not quite how life works. We need people in our lives. We need connection. In the movie *Cast Away*, Tom Hanks starts talking to his volleyball, which he names Wilson, out of sheer desperation to have some connection. As humans, we need connection.

In today's day and age of busy, our relationships are suffering. Relationships, whether with parents, children, spouses, or friends need tending to just like a garden. They need nourishment and time. I share with you now what's working for me.

With My Kids: I make an effort to be present for them. If they walk into my room and I'm on the computer, I close it. I put my phone down. I give them my full attention. This has been a hard one for me and is admittedly still a work in progress. But I want my kids to feel like they are more important than whatever is on my screen. I make sure to have one-on-one time with each kid. Plan a date with them. The dynamic is so different when they are alone.

With My Parents: I call. I visit. I occasionally write them a letter. I ask them to share stories from their past. Even as I write this, I realize I need to do more.

With My Friends: When my kids were little, I didn't do a ton with my friends. But I made an effort to set up girls night every quarter. I have some friends where we meet for long walks with our dogs. I have other friends who I meet for a glass of wine. Women especially love to connect and will get an oxytocin boost from communication and time together. Now that my kids are grown, my time for friendships has blossomed. This is now a big part of my life that I love.

With My Husband: I feel like I put the most work into this relationship. Maybe it's because we will be together forever, God-willing. Maybe because it's the hardest. We do a lot to work on our relationship. We read marriage books and listen to podcasts. We go to therapy. Some of the best things we have done include having a weekly catch-up meeting. This is not a date. It's a ten- to fifteen-minute weekly check-in. What's on the calendar? What's coming up? What do we need help with? We do a monthly planned date night where we switch off planning and try to plan a fun, unique night for the other. We have done things like cooking classes, concerts, picnics, and even hikes.

For all these, we need to set aside time for the relationship. We can't neglect them and then think they will be there. Some relationships need time each day. Some each week. Maybe some each quarter. But they need time. Our relationships need presence. Put down your devices. Turn off the TV. Look in each other's eyes. Make deposits. I think we got this idea from Stephen Covey. Pick a relationship to look at. Imagine a day with that person. How many deposits did you make? This could be a compliment, doing something for them, giving them a gift, touching them. How many withdrawals did you make? This could be a judgment, a nag, a complaint, raising one's voice, ignoring them. The goal is to make five deposits before you take a withdrawal.

COMMUNICATION

I'm learning the power behind my communication in my relationships. I am learning the value of having hard conversations. I used to try desperately to keep everyone happy and positive: no conflict. I thought no one should be fighting. I have learned that healthy conflict and candid conversations are critical for truly deep relationships. Being honest about our challenges is the only way to overcome them. Of course, there are ways to handle hard conversations in productive ways. I no longer desire for everyone to be happy all the time. I would prefer to have deep, honest relationships with the people I love.

I was surprised at the amount of work I have needed to put into better communication. I didn't think it was anything I had to work on. I'm a nice person after all. Boy, was I wrong. My communication has been the hardest thing for me to work on in my relationships. I found that I had no filter. I would say what was on my mind without taking a moment to think about how it would be received. Even if it was not my intention, my words were sometimes hurtful or put people on the defense, which was definitely *not* my goal. So I've been working on it. I read the book *Nonviolent Communication* by Marshall Rosenberg. I learned a lot about communication from the Gottman Method and even went to a Gottman Method therapist.

Here are some of the things that I'm working on. Most of these are specific to my marriage work, but they can be applied to almost any relationship.

Check In: One of the best things Jason and I did to improve our communication was a daily check-in. We ask each other what their emotional bank account balance is. In our home, we have a rule that our real bank accounts have to keep a minimum balance of $300. So if we tell the other person that our Emotional Bank Account is running at $250, they know it's low. Sometimes, we have to tell the other person that the account is overdrawn. It is a nice reminder to know how the other is doing and if they need a deposit.

Create the Space for Communication: When you are sooooo busy, it's hard to find the right time to have a real conversation. You might throw it in between dinner and dishes and find yourself exasperated and in a fight. One thing that has helped us is to have times set aside for communication. I mentioned the check-in above. But we also do a "happy hour" check-in. On days that I know we need to talk, I set aside a little time to sit down before dinner and have a conversation (and, yes, a glass of wine). When the kids were little, I would send them up to do homework or whatever to get out of our hair. I wish we did it more often. But I can tell you that when we do it, it works!

Soft Start-up: This is right out of the Gottman Method. It's better to bring up problems gently rather than just diving in. If you start a conversation by attacking your partner, you will pretty surely end your conversation in an argument.

Make Statements Like "I" instead of "You": It feels less critical and just shares that these are your feelings or your perception. Read the following statements and see how you would like to be approached.

"You are always on your phone. You never pay attention to me."

"I feel like we are not connected when the phone is holding your attention. I would love if you could put your phone down when we have a conversation."

Observe and Recap: This is from Nonviolent Communication practice. Start with a neutral observation. This is how you can respond when someone communicates something unpleasant to you. Maybe they just made a comment about politics that you find offensive. Instead of reacting, observe their stance and recap it: "I hear you saying that you are concerned about the immigrants." This slows down the conversation and lets the person know they were heard. From there you can respond with your feelings.

Listen, Listen, *Really* Listen: Most of us love to hear ourselves talk. We are so ready to respond that we don't really sit and listen to what the other person is saying. Practice listening to understand and not to respond. Repeat back what you heard to show that you are really listening and to ensure that they are understood. Then you can thoughtfully choose your response.

Silence: Yes, silence is part of your communication. Silence is a way that I avoided getting in fights or having conflict; I now know that it is very destructive. What happens is that you feel alone, isolated. You bury the wounds or whatever is bothering you, but they are still there. I now know that I have to speak up. Strangely, I have learned that it always brings us closer together. Keeping silent and just keeping things status quo is very much resignation. You will separate and feel a loss of connection. So, give yourself space; you can start small, but speak up.

I always thought relationships should come naturally. Basically, I didn't realize how much work needed to be put into them. You can't expect them to just happen.

VILLAGE HABITS

These are practices to track in your Level Up Journal. As always, this list is just meant to give you ideas for habits you can add to your life. Feel free to try these or come up with your own practices.

- Schedule a monthly date with your friends.
- Join a club or peer group.
- Spend ten minutes a day connecting with a family member.
- Hug your spouse or partner upon leaving and arriving for the day.
- Be a pen pal to someone.

As always, this list is just meant to give you ideas for habits you can add to your life.

Here is how this may look in your Level Up Journal:

	MON	TUE	WED	THU	FRI	SAT	SUN
Daily kiss with Hubby (goal: daily)	X	X	X	X	X	X	X
Call family (goal: weekly)			X				

PURPOSE

> "The two most important days in your life are the day
> you are born and the day you find out why."
>
> – MARK TWAIN

I now know that purpose is the foundation for me to have a meaningful life. Purpose is defined as the reason we do something or why something exists. It's your conviction for what you want to create in your life. I am talking about the intention to do something that is meaningful and will have a positive impact. You might say it's your "why" for being. When you are living in alignment with your values and beliefs, you are living with purpose.

What do you stand for?
What do you believe in?
Are you living in alignment with those values?

Scientists, researchers, and philosophers have always wondered: Is the meaning of life to be happy, or to find and serve your purpose? Is there even a difference? The thing that inspires me, that motivates me, is purpose. I have an incredible purpose behind my work at FIT4MOM. It fuels me and makes me want to stick with it even when it's hard. I have purpose in my marriage, my parenting, my health, my relationships. They are my *why*, and my why keeps me engaged in my life. My purpose has become my compass; my North Star. It helps me decide what I say yes to and what I say no to. I reconnect to it daily so that I know I'm on the right path. When I veer off of it, I come back.

I know that finding your purpose sounds big. It doesn't have to be a profound, "You're going to change the world," purpose. Your purpose might be to be a great parent. Your purpose might be something for a specific season of your life. For instance, at the time of writing this chapter, it's summer. My purpose recently has been guided by writing this book. I have pulled back on my work so I have more time. I could just enjoy summer. Kick back. Have fun. But, truthfully, I find myself very lost without a sense of purpose. Yes, I will enjoy the time and will play and relax, but my purpose for this summer is to write this book. It gives me a sense of direction for the day. It gives me some structure.

IKIGAI

Have you ever felt a lingering sense of longing, a yearning to find your place in the world? Perhaps you've wondered what your true purpose is, what unique contribution you can make to in this world. If so, you're not alone. Many of us crave a deeper sense of fulfillment, a clearer understanding of why we're here and what we're meant to do.

In the quaint village of Okinawa, Japan, nestled amidst the rolling hills and tranquil forests, lies a community with the highest density of centurions (people who live into their hundreds). One key factor is their diet; another is their lifestyle. Perhaps most importantly, Okinawans possess a deep sense of purpose and meaning in life: a concept closely aligned with a concept called "Ikigai" (pronounced Ih-kee-guy). Derived from the Japanese words 'iki' (life) and 'gai' (value or worth), Ikigai is often described as the intersection of what you love, what you're good at, what the world needs, and what you can be paid for. It's your reason for being, your guiding light in a world of uncertainty.

Picture a Venn diagram with four circles overlapping at the center. Each circle represents a different aspect of your life: passion, vocation, profession, and mission. When you find the convergence of these elements, you discover your Ikigai: a harmonious balance of joy, fulfillment, and purpose.

But how do you uncover your Ikigai?

First, take time to reflect on your passions. What activities bring you joy and fulfillment? What makes your heart sing and your spirit soar? Whether it's writing, painting, gardening, or cooking, pay attention to the activities that ignite your soul and fill you with a sense of purpose.

Next, explore your talents and strengths. What are you naturally good at? What skills do you possess that set you apart? Whether it's your creativity, analytical mind, or ability to empathize with others, embrace the unique gifts that make you who you are.

Then, consider the needs of the world around you. What problems or challenges resonate with you? Where do you see opportunities to make a positive impact? Whether it's addressing environmental issues, supporting underserved communities, or promoting mental health awareness, look for ways to align your passions with the needs of the world.

Finally, think about how you can translate your passions and talents into a viable profession. How can you create value for others while also supporting yourself financially? Whether it's starting a business, pursuing a career in a meaningful field, or freelancing in your area of expertise, explore opportunities to monetize your passions in a way that aligns with your values and goals.

As you embark on your Ikigai journey, remember that it's not always a linear path. There will be twists and turns, challenges and setbacks, moments of doubt and uncertainty. But through it all, stay true to yourself and trust in the process. Your Ikigai is waiting for you to uncover it, hidden in plain sight, ready to guide you on a journey of purposeful living.

So take the first step today. Reflect on what brings you joy, embrace your talents, and seek out opportunities to make a difference in the world.

WHAT YOU LOVE

Start with your heart. What are things you are passionate about? If you don't even know, pay attention to what you follow on social media. What conversations get you fired up? What topics do you love to talk about? What books are you drawn to? Feel it. What gets you excited? What makes you come alive? For instance, my feed in social media is made up of the following:

- Travel
- Food
- Exercise
- Mindset / Meditation
- Longevity Experts
- Menopause Experts (this is more recent)
- Entrepreneurism

Boom! A pretty perfect curation of what I'm passionate about. Yours might have house renovations, dogs, shopping. It's a pretty good indicator of what interests you.

Try things. I normally hate the word "try," but it works here. Try lots of different things. Take classes, try out new activities, take small steps towards something that interests you. Just take some action. If you are excited to work on it, you are on the right track. If you are dreading it, then you know it's not yours to do.

WHAT YOU ARE GOOD AT

If you aren't really sure what you are good at, think about what people come to you for. Maybe you are a master organizer or an incredible meal planner. Maybe people come to you because you make them laugh. Chances are, you are good at something (or many things), and that can lead you to your passionate purpose.

What makes you quirky or unique? The thing that you used to be embarrassed about (and maybe still are) might be the key to unlock your purpose. I already told you that I was a daydreamer. Well, I made my dreams come true. Now my team calls me an "idea monkey" (and I think it's a compliment).

WHAT THE WORLD NEEDS

Of course, the world needs a lot, from climate change to peace. But it doesn't have to be that big. What problems might you see a solution for? There are both problems and solutions everywhere. There are solutions that haven't even been thought of. I know a gal who was part of an online course. She saw that lots of people signed up but didn't follow through. She created another business where she held people accountable to go through the course. And she's super successful! What problem might you help solve?

I'm going to leave out the fourth element of ikigai, which is what people will pay for. That is important if you are looking for a passionate purpose that is also your career. But here I just want you to find your personal purpose that will add more meaning to your life. If you are lucky enough that it is also your work, then awesome!

Perhaps replace the fourth element with your values. What are your values? Don't just say what everyone thinks you should say. What do you *truly* value? What's most important to you? Family? Health? Freedom? Contribution? Again, your MITs really are your values.

So write down:

- What You Love
- What You Are Good At
- What the World Needs
- What Your Values Are

Where is there crossover? Don't force it. Just sit and be with it. It will come to you. To find your purpose, connect and contribute to something outside of yourself. Studies show that people are happiest when pursuing something with meaning. The pursuit of happiness is what thwarts happiness. Your purpose is something you would do for free (not that you have to).

My purpose when I became a mom was to find a career that could integrate with motherhood. That's when I started FIT4MOM. That purpose fueled me for years. That purpose evolved as I realized the impact that we made. My purpose became to create careers for other women that integrate with motherhood and to help women find their "fit in motherhood."

My purpose at FIT4MOM has now evolved as I want to make sure to create a diverse and inclusive environment for all moms. This purpose has created new challenges to overcome, but it keeps me inspired to figure out how to understand the maternal needs of BIPOC moms and figure out how we can create thriving and welcoming communities for them.

Your purpose is not always easy, but it will keep you driven towards progress. My purpose will continue to evolve with different seasons of life; but I will always find a purpose.

Ask retirees how they feel about losing a sense of purpose after the initial thrill of not working wears off. There is a very big problem among retirees of social isolation, depression, and not feeling needed. Some try to fulfill that by getting busy. Being busy is not the same as fulfillment. You don't have to go back to work. But you might want to learn something new. Volunteer or find ways to give back to your community. Keep growing.

A study from researchers at the University of California, San Diego, suggests that if you feel you have a purpose in life, you're more likely to feel both physically and mentally well on a daily basis. This doesn't mean that if you don't have a lofty purpose that you will be sick, but they found that people who have activities that are meaningful to them have found a source of well-being.

Imagine how your life would feel if you were purposeful about doing what you love, what you're good at, and what the world needs each day.

PURPOSE IN YOUR DAY

I am one of the few people I know who actually can relax and chill and do nothing for a day. Most of my friends and family don't know how to sit still. They feel lazy doing nothing. I am thrilled to sit and read a book or work in my garden, as that may be my purpose today. But we found through the pandemic that having no purpose in your day can be problematic.

During the pandemic, many people experienced disruptions to their daily routines, including changes in work, school, and social activities. With more time spent at home and fewer external commitments, some individuals found themselves lacking a sense of purpose or structure in their days. This lack of purpose could manifest as feelings of aimlessness, boredom, or even depression.

As people navigated these challenges, they began to recognize the importance of having a sense of purpose in their daily lives. Having a purpose provides direction, motivation, and a sense of fulfillment. It gives people a reason to get out of bed in the morning and helps them prioritize their time and energy.

Throughout the pandemic, individuals and communities experimented with various strategies to cultivate purpose and structure in their lives. This might include setting goals, pursuing hobbies or interests, volunteering, or finding new ways to connect with others. By actively engaging in activities that bring meaning and fulfillment, people discovered that they could maintain their well-being and resilience even in the face of uncertainty and adversity.

I am a huge goal setter. I set goals for the year. For the quarter. For the month. For the week. For the day. Remember, I have ADD, so it helps me to keep re-anchoring myself to my goals. Goals are really a purpose, aren't they? A goal is something we strive for that is aligned to a purpose. They support our purpose.

Each day, I ground myself to my purpose in the day. How do I want to show up? Who do I want to be as a leader, a mom, a wife? All of this is my purpose.

Your purpose may be simpler than you think. Some philosophers believe that "not being dead" is your purpose. If you're alive, it is meaningful!

PURPOSE HABITS

Here are some practices to track in your Level Up Journal. As always, this list is just meant to give you ideas for habits you can add to your life. I encourage you to try these or create your own.

- Start each day connecting to your purpose and what's important to you.
- Explore new interests each month. Discover what you love to do.

- Read self-development books or listen to podcasts.
- Journal or write in a daily diary.
- Ask yourself powerful questions each day.

How this may look in your Level Up Journal:

	MON	**TUE**	**WED**	**THU**	**FRI**	**SAT**	**SUN**
Listen to a podcast (goal: daily)	X	X	X	X	X		
Create and update a vision board (goal: weekly)							X

FUN, PLAY, ADVENTURE

> "We do not quit playing because we grow old,
> we grow old because we quit playing."
>
> **– OLIVER WENDELL HOLMES, SR.**

Now that we are in Chapter 9, I think we are close enough to the end that I can be honest with you. This chapter is the one that I feel least authentic to write about. I believe in it, 100 percent. But it's not something that comes naturally to me. I am not naturally really fun. I am introspective and purposeful. I am driven and like to work. Not really fun. So why am I including it? Because it's an ingredient in this recipe for the joy of living. I am purposeful to bring fun, play, and adventure into my life. I write this chapter not just for you, but also for me.

FUN

How do you define fun? Fun is defined as amusement, especially lively or playful. "Time flies when you're having fun." This saying implies that fun is freedom for us; it is a break from our routine. I suppose it's different for everyone. For me, gardening is fun. For others, it might be seen as tedious. For my daughter, shopping is fun. For me, not so much. For some moms, Target is fun. Again, for me, not so much. Ultimately, fun is about feeling happy, relaxed, and joyful.

It seems like people are not so inclined to have fun anymore. Maybe it's because of our over-commitment to work. Maybe it's because we feel like we should always be getting something done. We feel lazy or unproductive if we are having fun. Maybe you're not having fun because you feel like you don't have time for fun. Or maybe you're not having fun because you are afraid you'll look silly. For example, I think my husband would really enjoy dancing. I see a spark of joy when he dances a little at our house. But he doesn't dance, because he thinks he's not a good dancer and he'll look silly. You know what, honey? I say you should dance away! Maybe you're not having fun because you feel like it will cost money. Well, they say the best things in life are free, and fun falls into those things!

The fun we often have now is a form of escapism. We drink alcohol, we eat, we watch Netflix. Guilty here, too. Some people smoke. Some people shop online. But this isn't the kind of fun I'm seeking for us. You won't regret real fun, but you might regret one too many glasses of wine or wasting the day watching shows. The fun we often have now is lazy fun. It's easier to sit on the couch and watch Netflix (sorry, Netflix, for the continued callouts) then it is to go out and play pickleball or meet your friends for a walk. My experience is that we never regret the little bit of effort once we are out there.

I mentioned this in the chapter about our village: I now schedule fun. I have the following scheduled on my calendar:

- Monthly hike with friends
- Monthly game night with friends (Our favorites are Euchre, Azul, and Gin)
- Monthly walk and breakfast with other friends
- Quarterly lunch with other friends
- Monthly date night with Jason

Not all of my fun is scheduled around food or money. Spontaneous fun is equally a priority. When the kids were little, there were dance nights after dinner and tickle sessions. I played games in the backyard with the kids. Today, we are still finding ways to play and have fun. Jason and I play games almost every weekend (Gin is our favorite card game). Sometimes I turn on YouTube and do an African dance or to try to learn a line dance. I get on the ground and play with the dogs. And I'm still looking for more ways to have fun in my daily life.

When was the last time you had real fun? I invite you to think right now about all of the things that have been fun in your life. From vacations to playing piano. From going to a dog beach (one of my favorites) to playing board games with your kids (another one of my favorites). What has been fun for you? Are there things from your childhood that you remember as fun? Playing a sport? Doing puzzles? These things very well may still be a key for unlocking your fun factor. If you are looking for more ways to have fun, you might want to look to play.

At FIT4MOM, we have a Chief of Culture. Among other things, her job is to make sure we have fun at work. I of course needed to outsource this, since fun and play doesn't come naturally to me. But I'm always thrilled once we are doing it. At work, it can look like outings and retreats, games, challenges and contests, and shared experiences. When we take the fun out of work, it's just work.

PLAY

I have purposefully separated out fun and play. Fun is a natural byproduct of play. Play is not just for kids. There are libraries of books about how play is important for children's development. But play is also for us grown-ups. Play is a way for adults to have fun, relax, stimulate our brains, and spark creativity. But, somewhere along the way of growing up, we stopped playing.

I have two dogs. Every single day, every single night, they play. They chase and tag and wrestle. One signals to the other through a bark or a bow that it's time to play. And off they go. My dogs remind me to play every day. If I don't play with them, they bring me a ball. Every single day, they bring me a ball. Animals play their entire lives. People do not. We get bogged down in work and life, and we forget that play is what's missing in our joyful lives.

Remember when you were a kid and you just went out to play? Rode your bike? Jumped into a big pile of leaves? Played with friends? Played on the playground? Take a moment and really think back. When did you have the most fun as a kid? What was your favorite version of play?

We think that play is just for kids—but it's not.

When my kids were younger, it seemed easier. I danced with them. I played Red Light, Green Light with them. We played a lot more games. We wrestled and tickled. We told stories. But as they got older, the play faded.

The absence of play is harming us. Dr. Stuart Brown, founder and president of the National Institute for Play, says play lights up your brain, improves your mood, and connects you to the world. Play does a lot for the brain. Studies of the brain have shown that play deprivation shrinks the brain (and when it comes to the brain, bigger is better).

Play reduces stress.
Play increases endorphins which make you feel good (and lessen pain).
Play increases creativity.
Play helps our relationships.

So what can we do in our daily lives to bring more play and fun?

Dance.
Play a game.
Tell a joke.
Flirt.
Color or paint.
Craft.
Pick up a hobby.
Play a sport.
Go to the beach.
Go on a hike.
Go out with friends.
Wrestle with each other.

Looking at Facebook or TikTok is not play.

How do you define play? Some say play is what children do when they are not being told what to do by adults. A better definition might be, "A physical or mental leisure activity that is undertaken purely for enjoyment or amusement and has no other objective." What feels like play to you might not feel like play to someone else. It's yours. It should feel good. Ideally, it should be fun and even make you laugh. Exercise can be play. But if it feels like work, then it's really not.

ADVENTURE

> "Jobs fill your pockets, but adventures fill your soul."
> – JAIME LYN

Life is meant to be an adventure. Our lives are meant to be more than going to work and living the same routine day in and day out. Our lives were not meant to be lived on the couch. Our lives don't have to be boring. I'm not saying you need to climb Mt Everest or heli-ski down a mountain. But I am going to encourage you to look for mini adventures in your life. We should play, explore, and experience what this world has to offer.

When my kids were little, we used to go on "Mommy Adventures." We did this on days that their dad had to work. We would hop in the car, and they had no idea where we were going. The truth was—I also had no idea where we were going. I would choose a direction and just go. They even came up with a theme song for our adventures. We went to a cave in La Jolla, a roller coaster in Mission Bay, a children's museum, and more. Sometimes we would do multiple things in one day. A quick stop here and then a surprise stop there. It was light and fun and unexpected each time.

Ask my family about their favorite memories, and they will 100 percent say our vacations. They will then tell you about river rafting, zip lining, ATV rides, and swimming with dolphins. When we do these things, we are 100 percent filled with joy. We are in the moment and not on our phones. We are connected.

Of course, every day cannot be a vacation with thrills and adventure, but we can bring fun into our daily life. Watch a sunset. Go on a hike. If you live where there's a beach, go surf. If you live in the snow, go skiing. If you live near a lake, rope swing into it! Be a tourist in your own town and check out the sites. Try a new restaurant. Go on a roller coaster. Have a bonfire on the beach. I give you my blessing to use your phone, as there is probably an Instagrammer who covers the local adventures in your town. Maybe some of these things don't fit your definition of adventure. But I think if it's breaking you out of your rut and routine, then it is adventurous!

Curiosity is a great clue for your adventures. What are you curious about? Are you curious about national parks? Are you curious about a culture? A food? A place?

Do something new. Take a new route home. Go to a new restaurant. Try to learn a new language. Take up a new hobby. New experiences are adventures.

For me, adventure usually takes place outdoors. We know that the outdoors is full of benefits for our health and psyche. Nature will boost your mood and energy. For me, an adventure gets me disconnected from that little device that texts and dm's. For me, adventure scares me, excites me, or inspires me.

Psychologist James Loehr, EdD, co-founder of the Human Performance Institute in Orlando, says, "Our research shows that the ability to just view life as a hope-filled, exhilarating adventure represents a tremendous happiness and health advantage."

I said that it doesn't have to be anything risky. And it doesn't. But I will say that the few risks I have taken for adventure are for sure highlights of my life. I have ridden duckies (small kayaks) in rapids and repelled down waterfalls with my family . I skydived with my son and husband for their respective eighteenth and fiftieth birthdays. I was afraid of these things, but I left feeling exhilarated and also proud of having faced my fears. I felt alive! When you do something exciting, your brain triggers your nervous system to pump out the feel-good hormone, dopamine, along with endorphins that give you a natural high. It's not so much about risk but just getting out of your comfort zone.

Researchers have shown that life is more enjoyable when we are learning new things. Adventure can simply be trying new things. Studies have connected curiosity and being open to new experiences with a sharper mind. You are challenging your brain and creating new neural connections to stave off cognitive decline and Alzheimer's disease.

Think of things that use to bring you joy as a child. I think of playing Candy Land. Riding bikes in the cul-de-sac. Coloring in coloring books. Chances are that a version of these things will still bring joy to your life today. We just need to make sure to do them.

Here are some practices to track in your Level Up Journal. As always, this list is just meant to give you ideas for habits you can add to your life. You are encouraged to try any of these or make up your own.

- Start a hobby.
- Have a game night once a week.
- Plan a vacation.
- Do one new thing a month.
- Create a bucket list.
- Start a dinner club with friends.
- Start playing a sport like Pickleball.

- Play with your kids at the playground.
- Do something spontaneous.
- Dance after dinner.
- Do something that scares you.
- Have a dance party after dinner.
- Go to a comedy club.
- Be a tourist in your own city.
- Try a new restaurant.
- Go to the beach or the park.
- Ride a bike or go roller skating.

How this may look in your Level Up Journal:

	MON	TUE	WED	THU	FRI	SAT	SUN
Game night (goal: weekly)				X			
Dinner club (goal: monthly)	X						

BE ADDICTED TO GROWING YOURSELF

"Your number one job is to become more of yourself
and to grow yourself into the best of yourself."

– OPRAH WINFREY

The last chapter may have been the one that I felt least authentic about writing. This is the chapter I feel most authentic about writing. I am addicted to personal development. I once was asked in an interview to name my number one habit for success. My answer without hesitation was "intentional growth."

We all grow naturally. Kids physically grow up without trying. We grow just by living and gaining new experiences. But this is not enough. I am talking about *intentional* growth. Purposeful learning.

I am a self-development junkie. My friend Carey bought me a self-help book for people who read too many self-help books. I set aside time for learning every single day, mainly via audiobooks and podcasts. I walk my dogs and listen to an audiobook. I get ready in the morning and listen to a podcast. Drive and listen. Do dishes and listen. Instead of the radio or a TV making noise in the background, I listen and learn. Beyond that, I go to conferences and take online courses. You probably don't even know what is out there to support you in your learning. Go over to Google and search what you are looking for. Search the words "course," "conference," "mastermind," "podcast," and see what comes up.

The more I learn, the deeper becomes my reservoir for ideas, confidence to handle situations, and capacity for relationships. I can both love and appreciate the life I have now *and* desire to learn and grow more each day.

> Side note: Go to www.levelupyourlifebook.com for a list of my favorite podcasts and books.

The actual daily growth habits bring me joy in living each day. We find joy when we experience success but also when we develop our skills and mindset. The habit of intentional growth also brings satisfaction, because we all want to have control over our lives. Learning and growth has the potential to open doors and give you confidence about your life's direction. By being purposeful with my growth habits, I gain inspiration and new tools for all areas of my life. Whatever part of my life is feeling low—finance, relationships, health, work—I learn about. You can learn from the best of the best and gain valuable wisdom and insight.

GROWTH MINDSET

I obtained my master's degree is in psychology because I'm obsessed with our minds and how we can change them. Funnily enough, we have learned more about the brain and how it can change since I have left school. A prime example is the concept of growth mindset found in Carol Dweck's book *Mindset*. Basically, the concept is that there are two mindsets: fixed and growth. They are your perception about yourself. A fixed mindset is static and set. A growth mindset can be developed and changed. If you believe yourself to be fixed, you are going to be stuck. If you have a fixed mindset, you believe that intelligence and talent are set and there's not much you can do about it. Most people with a fixed mindset are reluctant to change or to learn. People with a fixed mindset tend to live in fear, defensiveness, and despair, because they feel they can't change their situation.

If you have a growth mindset, however, you believe that you can develop through hard work and dedication. You see your shortcomings and look for ways to make improvements. This is where you start to view challenges as opportunities. People with growth mindsets tend to be happier and more satisfied with their lives.

As a kid, I didn't feel very smart. I didn't feel very confident. My fixed mindset kept me stuck there. It wasn't until I started working hard to change that I realized I was not stuck. I could change. When I'm pursuing growth, I am happy.

Remember earlier when I shared the statement, "I'll be happy when _____." I have started to realize that it's not the destination that makes us happy. It is the journey towards those things.

Do you have a fixed mindset? Are you worried you are stuck there? The good news is that you are not stuck with a fixed mindset. You can expose yourself through learning to new ways of thinking. Remember when we talked about the thoughts you have each day? When you hear a fixed thought, do it over. For example:

Thought: I'm not good at math.
Do-over thought: I could be good at math if I put some work into it.

Thought: I'm not a good parent.
Do-over thought: I am exactly the mother my children need.

THE DEVELOPMENT ZONE

Of course we grow from every experience we have. The more experiences you have, the more you grow. Try new things. Every time you face a fear, you grow. Say yes to new opportunities, new challenges, and new experiences to help you on your path to growth.

Successful people grow on purpose. Learning never stops. Warren Buffet spends 80 percent of his time reading. Bill Gates carries around a tote bag of books that he replenishes weekly. The wisest and most successful people read. They read a *lot*! Oprah Winfrey says books were her path to personal freedom.

Why do we think that learning just happens in school? Why would we think it ends there? Go back to your Wheel of Life activity. What area were you not satisfied with? That is an area to hone in on and plan for growth.

1 PERCENT IMPROVEMENT

Most of us want to grow in a quantum leap. We want to lose five pounds this week. We want success by tomorrow. But growth happens via daily commitment and daily habits; it happens when little bits of progress begin to add up. Because I used to get overwhelmed by big projects or tasks, I would break them down into small habits. Each day, I would think about how I could do it 1 percent more or 1 percent better. Think about it: a 1 percent improvement is still growth. And a 1 percent improvement every day is 100 percent better in less than a third of a year. I use the 1 percent rule all day long.

The point of this book is to find the joy in living your daily life. Because of my ADD, I have learned that small habits done each day are less overwhelming than big drastic changes. Your small improvements each day are rewarding. Success begets success. You will feel good knowing you are directionally correct towards your goal. My brother-in-law is a pilot. I once asked him how often they are off track when they fly. He said there is never a perfect track. They are a little over and a little under. They keep coming back until they get to their destination. So why do we expect to be on a perfect track? Just stay directionally correct.

When I drop my clothes on the floor, I remind myself I can do 1 percent better and put them away. That small action is rewarding, like I checked a box. Not doing it would mean a floor filled with clothes, which would be distressing later. When I want to end my workout early, I choose to do a few minutes more. When I want to order something decadent, I challenge myself to make a better choice. Not the best choice— just a better choice. This decision to do 1 percent more can be a habit, and it is one that will prove fruitful in the present and in the long run.

Have you heard of Kaizen? It's the Japanese philosophy of continuous improvement. Kai means "change," and Zen means "good." It focuses on continual, incremental improvement. One of the most notable features of Kaizen is that big results come from many small changes, which build up over time. Instead of trying to make radical changes all at once, focus on making small changes each day. Sudden, dramatic life changes aren't sustainable or realistic. Instead, small changes will become the fabric of your life.

The spirit of Kaizen is reflected in the mighty ocean being made up of tiny drops of water. This does not mean that Kaizen brings small changes. You can apply it to any part of your life from knowledge to fitness, from parenting to business. What big change could you create by taking a small step towards it every day? Dream big, but then break it down. What is the next step? What small step could you take daily towards your goal? You don't have to have every step figured out. Just take the next step. And then the next day, take the next step.

Really, what you are doing is building new habits (the premise of this book). A Stanford researcher named B.J. Fogg is an expert on habit formation. Part of his research focused on how to get people to floss their teeth. The answer was one tooth at a time. They told the subjects to just floss one tooth when they brushed their teeth. That was do doable, so they complied. And so they built a habit—and started flossing them all.

One of the reasons they believe this works is because we have a dissonance with starting something new. As I mentioned, my master's degree is in psychology, so I love this stuff. I'm fascinated with how we need to trick the brain. It's called the Zeigarnik effect. A psychologist named Bluma Zeigarnik found you are less likely to procrastinate once you start doing a task. So I'm telling you to start, no matter how small the task is.

Writing this book is a giant project. But I'm not tackling it all at once. I take a Kaizen approach and work on just a little bit at a time.

GROWTH AND DEVELOPMENT
Here are some practices to track in your Level Up Journal. As always, this list is just meant to give you ideas for habits you

can add to your life. You are encouraged to try any of these or make up your own.

- Take an online course.
- Go to a conference or event.
- Listen to a podcast.
- Read a book.
- Set aside some time each week for personal development or learning.
- Find a mentor.

How this may look in your Level Up Journal:

	MON	**TUE**	**WED**	**THU**	**FRI**	**SAT**	**SUN**
Listen to a podcast (goal: workdays)	X	X	X	X	X		
Set aside an hour for learning (goal: weekly)					X		

THE GIFT OF GIVING

> "If you want happiness for an hour, take a nap. If you want happiness for a day, go fishing. If you want happiness for a year, inherit a fortune. If you want happiness for a lifetime, help somebody."
>
> **– CHINESE PROVERB**

We've all heard the saying that it's better to give than to receive. In fact, the concept of helping others being good for you has been around for thousands of years. Aristotle wrote that finding happiness and fulfillment is achieved "by loving rather than in being loved." Yet, today, we live in a very "selfie" world, a world where we focus a lot on ourselves.

Perhaps we have forgotten the gift of giving because we feel depleted. I know as a mom, it feels like all we do is give. I'm guessing dads and, well, really all adults feel this way. At work, you might feel like you give all you've got and you have nothing left to give. You feel like your giving reservoir is dry. But this is not the kind of giving I'm talking about. The kind of giving I'm talking about will not deplete you; it will benefit you as much as the recipient.

At times when I have felt low, I have focused on giving as a pathway to feeling better. The truth is that our brain is wired for giving. It literally lights up when we give. Humans are social creatures. We are wired to help each other. Quite literally. When we give, we create happy hormones like serotonin, dopamine, and oxytocin. It's like altruism is hard-wired in our brains. When you give to someone, your brain lights up in the same way as if you were the receiver of the giving. The dose of oxytocin after giving can last for up to two hours. So a simple act of giving can cause a feeling of wanting to continue giving.

I have donated my time at various food banks in San Diego over the years. Admittedly, the thought of going often feels like an inconvenience. I'm already so busy as a business owner and mom. But every single time I go, I am so happy that I'm there, and for hours afterwards I feel a warm fuzzy feeling. I am far more likely to sign up to go again during this time. It's like a domino effect of giving. You want to keep giving.

I could probably make a bigger impact for these charities with a financial donation. But, selfishly, donating my time is good for me too. I feel so grateful for my own life, and I feel good about donating my time.

There is an unbelievable amount of research showing that giving is good for our health, our relationships, our wealth, and our life.

GIVING IS GOOD FOR YOUR HEALTH

Stephen Post is the author of *Why Good Things Happen to Good People*. He is a professor of preventive medicine at Stony Brook University. His findings show health benefits of giving for people with chronic illness, including HIV and multiple sclerosis. He also found that generous behavior is closely associated with reduced risk of illness, mortality, and depression.

Carnegie Mellon University published a study in *Psychology and Aging* that people who volunteer are less likely to have high blood pressure than those who do not. Lower blood pressure is associated with lower chance of health problems, including heart disease and stroke.

Giving will help you live longer; the research is astounding. Various studies show that those who help consistently live longer. Proceedings of the National Academy of Science indicate a linear relationship between amount and frequency of wealth transfers and length of life. It's no wonder that Mother Teresa lived to 87 and Mahatma Gandhi lived to 78! Miep Gies, the amazing woman who helped protect Anne Frank and her family, as well as helped many others in need, lived to 100!

GIVING IMPROVES OUR RELATIONSHIPS AND SOCIAL CONNECTION

Think about it. The more you give, the more you get back. This connection improves our trust and cooperation with others. It makes us feel closer to people. Having strong social connections helps both our happiness and feeling of purpose. Even when you give to a charity, it helps you feel more connected to the world. Giving can also expand your relationships. You will build connections with those you help; you will also build connections with the other helpers.

I found early in my business that moms have a shared desire to make the world better for their kids. We started our Moms With A Mission program in the early years of FIT4MOM. Nationwide, moms come together for a variety of causes. We raise money, raise awareness, and volunteer for local and national charities. The experiences bring us closer together as moms and model to our kids a lifetime of philanthropic work.

I mentor students at the local university. I benefit greatly from the connection with my mentees. My mentees give me fresh perspective from the life of a college student. It's incredibly rewarding to see mentees go off into their careers, knowing you may have given them just a little direction. Whenever I mentor, I gain valuable insight and support from my fellow mentors. It's incredible to surround yourself with other successful people who also have a heart to help others.

GIVING IMPROVES GRATITUDE

Helping others puts your life in perspective. Perhaps you are helping someone in need. You may realize that your problems are small in comparison, or you are grateful that you have a gift or time to share. Scientists also believe that altruistic behavior releases endorphins in the brain, producing the positive feeling known as the "helper's high."

TYPES OF GIVING

Not all types of giving will have the benefits mentioned above. If you feel forced to give, it will not light up the brain. If you have an automatic financial donation, it will probably not have the same benefits as the moment you decide to write a check or give money to someone in need. My family "adopted" a child in Africa. It's been over a dozen years. The charge just automatically comes on my credit card. I'm glad we are doing it, but the feel-good part has dissipated. Buying a gift for someone who is expecting it will probably not feel as good as surprising someone with an unexpected gift.

Here are some ways to give that will also be a gift to you.

Time: One of our most precious resources is time. It's the one thing we can't create more of. So, when you give your time, it's a pretty special gift. Taking time away from work, friends, and our own leisure time seems arduous. But every time we go, we all are so glad we did it. It feels good to give. It also catapults our gratitude for our own lives. We don't all have money to give, but time is a resource that we all can choose to spend. Other ways I volunteer my time are giving blood, mentoring. and volunteering at my kids' schools (when they were younger). I am not saying this to put a feather in my cap. Truly, each one of these activities gives as much to me as to the people I'm helping.

Money: Laura Aknin did a study where they gave a twenty-dollar bill (sometimes other amounts) to a person. In one sample, they told people to spend the money on themselves. In another, they told them to spend it on someone else. The people who spent on someone else were happier than those who spent it on themselves. Giving money alone will probably not light up your brain with benefits. You need to find something that is meaningful to you. In my family, our kids had to give a percentage of their allowance to savings and a percentage to charity. As a family, we would pick the charities that we wanted to donate to. According to Harvard scientist Michael Norton, "Giving to a cause that specifies what they're going to do with your money leads to more happiness than giving to an umbrella cause where you're not so sure where your money is going." Paying for the person behind you at the coffee shop will probably make you feel good too.

Passion: We talked in an earlier chapter about finding your passion. You are more likely to benefit from giving when it's tied to something you care about. When you care about who you are giving to, you are more likely to experience the benefits of giving.

Proactive Giving: You are more likely to experience joy from giving when you initiate it. It is less enjoyable when you feel cajoled into donating to a charity or giving your time. It's still good, and it's still a benefit to the receiver. But you will feel better and have a warm, glowy feeling when you are the one who initiates the giving.

Tomato Surprise: A dear friend of mine used to leave us "Tomato Surprises." This could be a small candle, a pretty pen, a new Chapstick. It was just a little something to surprise and delight. She once gave a Tomato Surprise to my daughter, and they went back and forth for years leaving each other little gifts. It gave them such joy. Honestly, it gave me joy just to watch them.

It may seem like people are selfish, but truly we are a generous species. A gift doesn't have to be grand. You don't want to be guilted into giving. Find ways to give that feel good to you. Start small and see how good it feels.

GIVING

Here are some practices to track in your Level Up Journal. As always, this list is just meant to give you ideas for habits you can add to your life. You are encouraged to try any of these or make up your own.

- Volunteer.
- Make a donation.
- Help a neighbor in need.
- Buy coffee for the person behind you.
- Surprise someone with an unexpected gift.
- Mentor.
- Give blood.
- Start a meal train for a family or a mom in need.
- Tutor.
- Coach.
- Support a social cause.
- Help a neighbor.

How this may look in your Level Up Journal:

	MON	TUE	WED	THU	FRI	SAT	SUN
Random act of kindness (goal: weekly)					X		
Volunteer						X	

GET OUTSIDE

*"In every walk with nature, one
receives far more than he seeks."*

– JOHN MUIR

In recent years, I have come up with five daily rules for myself. 1) Move daily. 2) Eat mainly whole foods. 3) Meditate. 4) Practice gratitude. 5) Get outside—and ideally not just outside, but I want my feet to hit dirt.

This chapter is about how nature brings joy into your daily life.

I live in San Diego, an amazing place to be outside. Yet, for many, many years I spent most of my time indoors. You wake up, work, eat your meals, go to bed. It never crossed my mind that I hadn't seen the sky. My life was confined to my home. You know what got me outside? My dogs. Well, first, dog singular. Dogs need walks. I started to realize that being outside recharged me. It refreshed me. More was better. I realized that getting outside needed to be one of my daily habits.

VITAMIN N: THE BENEFITS OF NATURE

Nature really is the best medicine. A new scientific field called ecotherapy is resulting in a great deal of research showing the connection between time spent in nature and the following health benefits:

Decreased stress
Lowered blood pressure
Increased happiness
Increased Vitamin D
Improved memory
Reduced inflammation
Reduced fatigue
Improved focus
Increased creativity

And guess what: It's free! A study published in the *International Journal of Environmental Health Research* said that spending twenty minutes a day at a park will increase your well-being. Exercising outside is great, but you don't even have to exercise to have benefits. Researchers from the University of Exeter Medical School in the United Kingdom found benefits to being outside for two hours per week, and it didn't matter how that time was broken up.

Researchers aren't exactly sure why nature has such positive impacts on the brain. Here's what we do know: The prefrontal cortex is a part of the brain that "malfunctions" when people are stressed or depressed. It is highly active with a continuous loop of negative thoughts. When people go on a nature walk, their prefrontal cortex has lower activity.

Doctors are starting to write "nature prescriptions,"

encouraging their patients to get outdoors. Doctors in Scotland have created calendars with prompts to encourage patients to get outdoors. Dr. Robert Zarr, a pediatrician based in Washington, D.C., helped establish Park Rx America to decrease chronic disease—and increase health and happiness—through spending time in nature.

THE INDOOR GENERATION

We are the indoor generation. We spend 90 percent of our time indoors without enough daylight or fresh air. We are nature-deprived. People spend their days under fluorescent lights looking at their phones, their computers, their televisions. By 2050, 66 percent of the world's population is projected to live in cities. According to a study sponsored by the Environmental Protection Agency, the average American spends 93 percent of his or her time indoors.

The Indoor Generation is a campaign that succeeded in creating global awareness of how indoor environment affects your health and well-being. They engaged NGOs, politicians, industry stakeholders, and consumers across forty-one countries. They say we have gone from being a part of nature to being *apart from* nature. We live in a time where technology is constantly pulling our attention. Our brains were not made for this bombardment of information. Nature helps relieve this kind of fatigue. It seems that the higher our stress, the less time we spend in nature. But maybe we are more stressed because we aren't getting in nature.

We don't think about it anymore. Even when we go outdoors, our feet hit cement. We have forgotten that nature is healing. While I am writing this chapter, we are still in the midst of a pandemic. When COVID-19 first hit, many of us got outside more because we were under stay-at-home orders. Never before have I seen so many families taking walks or on family bike rides. It was so nice. But it feels like that novelty has worn off, and now we are all just inside. We aren't even getting outside to go to the office. We just sit in our homes, looking at screens.

It's so easy to be inside all the time. There's nothing we lack when we're indoors. For most of us, it's pretty comfortable inside—and we are all addicted to comfort. Most of us also have jobs that require us to be indoors. How many of us work in an office, seeing only fluorescent lights for eight to ten hours per day? Some people get to the office before the sun rises and leave after it sets, never getting the benefits of sunshine.

I have learned that nature is the best medicine. If you work in an office, make it a point to take breaks and get outside. If it's snowing outside, bundle up. Even a few minutes of fresh air will do you good. If it's raining, grab an umbrella and don't forget to jump in a puddle.

Since the pandemic started, I have worked at home. As mentioned, every morning I take my dogs for a walk outside. On most days, I veer off the sidewalk and hit a nearby trail. I take two to three breaks during my workday. I go outside and water my garden. I pick up dog poop in the backyard (not exciting, but still in nature). I will often bring my computer in my backyard for work or take a call on a walk. We can take advantage of our technology. On weekends, I spend a lot of time outside. Yes, I acknowledge I live in San Diego and so it's a lot easier to do this. I go for runs, hike with the dogs, go to farmers markets. My husband teases me that I chase the sun. Our backyard only gets sun for a handful of hours during the day in winter. I move my chair around and chase the sun as I sit and read or work. (Yes, I wear sunblock). Or sometimes, I just sit. You should see what happens when the outside becomes more of your home. These habits of daily nature escaped me before. I would work twelve-hour days, never getting a moment of fresh air. This habit change has been life-changing for me.

It's probably not a surprise that the countries with the happiest people have the most beautiful natural environments. I'm talking about Costa Rica, New Zealand, and Finland. Urban jungles are rarely mentioned.

The *best* vacations I have ever taken have been based on the outdoors.

Snowboarding in Tahoe

River rafting in Costa Rica

Snorkeling in Mexico

Chilling at the lake in Big Bear

When do you get outdoors? Weekends? Vacations? An occasional scenic drive? Getting outside daily is an easy and free prescription to help you enjoy your life.

Feel the sun on your face.

Feel the breeze.

The crisp of the morning air.

Come on: You don't need a study to tell you that being in nature feels so good.

My friend Rebecca Cohen wrote the book *Fifteen Minutes Outside: 365 Ways to Get Out of the House and Connect with Your Kids*. She provides ideas for every day to get your family outside. I live in San Diego where it's easy to go outdoors year round. Rebecca also shares activities you can do in the snowiest of weather. You will find new ways to connect with your kids, get them off of devices, and back into nature.

BRING THE OUTSIDE IN

Nothing beats the real thing. However, research shows that you can have benefits from bringing nature inside. Researchers used an MRI scanner to check brain activity when people listen to sounds recorded from natural or artificial environments. Listening to natural sounds showed brain activity associated with dreams and focus. Listening to artificial sounds showed more brain activity associated with anxiety and stress.

Other ways to bring nature in are to surround yourself with plants, indoor fountains, and open windows. Hospitals have found that simply bringing a plant into a hospital room can decrease patient stress and increase wellness. Believe it or not, it is even beneficial to look at pictures of nature. Consider making your home screen of your computer a soothing nature scene.

FOREST BATHING

I fell in love the first time I heard this term. You won't need a suit for this kind of bathing. In Japan, there is a practice called forest bathing, or "shinrin-yoku." In 1982, the Ministry of Agriculture, Forestry and Fisheries of Japan instituted a national forest bathing program and has since designated a number of regional forest bathing reserves. It was created as a solution to the tech burnout and overload of its people.

It is simply about being in nature with all of your senses. It's a way to slow down and immerse yourself in your natural environment. The goal is to be present in nature. You can forest bathe anywhere in the world. All you need is nature… and some trees. You could do this at your local park.

Leave your phone behind. Take a few deep cleansing breaths. What are your senses taking in?

Pay attention to the sounds. Birds chirping, leaves rustling.

Pay attention to the sights. The color of the leaves and the sky, the sway of branches.

Pay attention to the smells. The smell of grass, of the air.

Touch. Feel the roughness of the bark on a tree. The coolness of the blade of grass.

Taste. I suppose if you are in a forest with some fruit trees or berry bushes you could taste the fruit. Maybe you want to mindfully eat your lunch while sitting in the park. You can mindfully walk or just sit. Just be.

People are getting certified as forest bathing guides. There are now forty years of research showing the benefits of forest bathing, including lower blood pressure, decreased stress, and improved energy.

Perhaps your job doesn't afford you this much flexibility, or your weather doesn't permit you to get outside. I will share more ideas on how to bring nature and light indoors.

Most of us spend more time at work than anywhere else. Research shows that natural elements and indirect sunlight correlate positively to job satisfaction and organizational commitment and negatively to anxiety and depressed mood. Employees with views to natural elements experience lower blood pressure, lower anxiety, and less depression. They have increased psychological well-being and fewer sick days. Researchers believe that these natural elements have a calming effect on physiology. You can do this through plants, pictures of nature, and window views. In a day and age where we are struggling to keep our workforce and to keep them healthy, I think these things are worth considering. Employees naturally experience stressors at work; however, those are experienced less when employees are in workspaces with more natural environments. Sunlight is highly correlated with employee mood. In fact, it is rated more importantly than the natural elements in the office. If you are in an office that does not have sunlight, encourage regular breaks where employees get outside to get some fresh air.

NATURE

Here are some practices to track in your Level Up Journal. As always, this list is just meant to give you ideas for habits you can add to your life.

- Take a daily walk.
- Go on a weekend hike.
- Go on a bike ride.
- Participate in an outdoor sport.
- Do yoga or meditate outdoors.
- Plant a garden.
- Surround your home with houseplants.
- Have pictures of nature around you.
- Go fishing.
- Go to a farmers market.
- Go on a picnic.
- Get fresh flowers for your house.
- Plant an indoor herb garden.
- Play nature music while you work.
- Go kayaking or boating.

How this may look in your Level Up Journal:

	MON	TUE	WED	THU	FRI	SAT	SUN
Take a walk outside (goal: daily)	X	X	X	X	X	X	X
Work in the garden (goal: 3x a week)	X		X			X	

EMBRACING SPIRITUALITY

"True religion is real living; living with all one's soul,
with all one's goodness and righteousness."

– ALBERT EINSTEIN

This chapter was originally not in this book. I teach what I know, or have figured out. I am not a very religious person and in fact have some ambivalence around religion, so it felt hypocritical to include this chapter. I also know that religion can be divisive, which is the last thing I want in this book. Yet I realized that most everything I do is through my connection to spirit, and many of my happiest friends have religion and spirituality as foundational in their lives. So it now seems very fitting to wrap up this book with this topic. This chapter explores how you can incorporate elements of religion and spirituality into your life to enhance your well-being.

I should first start with honesty and where I have trouble with religion. It seems throughout history and in current times that so much division has been created by religion. People assume their god is the right one, that their practice is the right one. There is little tolerance around people's differences. When I was in college, my roommate's very Christian sister told me that she was so sad that I would be going to hell, because I was Jewish and hadn't let Christ into my heart. I was so taken aback. I still have trouble understanding how people can be so literal about their religion.

While in college, I took a world religions course. It was actually one of my favorite classes. In fact, I felt like this was how everyone should choose a religion: learn about them and choose what feels aligned with your values. In this case, I would probably have chosen Buddhism. What I learned was that the heart of all religion is essentially the same. We might disagree on God and an afterlife, but most religions share similar moral values such as love, respect, and peace. What all religions offer is community, purpose, meaning, and hope.

In 1961, the *Saturday Evening Post* shared this by Norman Rockwell: "I'd been reading up on comparative religion. The thing is that all major religions have the Golden Rule in Common. 'Do unto others as you would have them do unto you.' Not always the same words but the same meaning."

In the pursuit of happiness, many people find solace and joy through religion and spirituality. These concepts, though intertwined, are not identical. Religion often refers to an organized system of beliefs and practices, while spirituality is a more personal and individualized experience. Both can significantly contribute to one's happiness by providing a sense of purpose, community, and inner peace.

UNDERSTANDING THE ROLE OF RELIGION AND SPIRITUALITY

Religion and spirituality offer a framework for understanding life's complexities, coping with difficulties, and finding meaning. Studies have shown that individuals who engage in religious or spiritual practices often report higher levels of happiness and life satisfaction. This is partly because these practices provide a sense of belonging and a connection to something greater than oneself.

I am Jewish. This has meant different things at different times of my life. As a child, we didn't go to temple, yet we always took off on the high holidays and spent the day together as a family. Mom always cooked a holiday meal, and we were together. We did our own abbreviated version of the Passover Sedar. I never knew any differently, and I never considered what else it might look like.

When my son was a pre-teen, I decided that he was going to get a bar mitzvah. I never had a bat mitzvah, but I was hoping that it would give Jacob a sense of connection to Judaism. I was hoping it would be something he would be proud of. I was proud of him. But for him, it didn't create a connection.

As an adult woman with grown kids, I am still trying to figure out my connection to religion. I appreciate the traditions, the culture, and more than anything the shared memories of the holidays. I am hoping my children find their own connection to spirituality or religion, because there are many benefits.

THE PSYCHOLOGICAL BENEFITS

Engaging in religious or spiritual activities can have profound psychological benefits. According to research, these practices can reduce stress, anxiety, and depression. This is because they often encourage mindfulness, reflection, and a sense of peace. Furthermore, having a belief system can help individuals navigate life's challenges by providing hope and resilience.

Religious and spiritual practices often promote positive coping mechanisms. Many religious teachings emphasize forgiveness, gratitude, and compassion, which can improve interpersonal relationships and reduce negative emotions. Engaging in rituals, prayers, or meditation can also create a structured time for individuals to reflect, process emotions, and find inner calm.

Religion and spirituality can also offer a sense of purpose and meaning in life. Believing in a higher power or a greater purpose can give individuals a sense of direction and motivation, which is particularly beneficial during times of adversity. This sense of meaning can enhance overall life satisfaction and contribute to a more optimistic outlook.

The moral and ethical guidelines provided by many religions can serve as a framework for making decisions and handling life's challenges. These guidelines can help individuals feel more confident and secure in their choices, reducing the uncertainty and stress that often accompany difficult decisions.

The rituals and traditions associated with religious practices can provide a comforting sense of continuity and stability. In times of change or crisis, these familiar practices can be grounding and reassuring, helping individuals to cope with uncertainty and maintain a sense of normalcy.

THE SOCIAL ASPECT

Religion and spirituality often foster a sense of community. Being part of a group that shares your values and beliefs can create a strong support system. This sense of belonging is crucial for emotional well-being. Communities provide emotional support, practical help, and a space for sharing experiences, which can significantly enhance your quality of life. Being part of a supportive community can reduce feelings of isolation and loneliness, which are common contributors to mental health issues.

BUILDING A SPIRITUAL COMMUNITY

A spiritual community can provide support, encouragement, and a sense of belonging. Whether it's a religious congregation, a meditation group, or a book club focused on spiritual texts, finding a community that shares your values can enhance your spiritual journey.

Join a group. Look for groups in your area that focus on spirituality or personal growth. This could be a yoga class, a meditation group, or a religious organization. Being part of a group can provide a sense of accountability and support.

SPIRITUAL TRADITIONS AND RITUALS

I am not particularly religious, as I mentioned, but I do appreciate traditions and rituals. We had our own traditions that we looked forward to. On Yom Kippur, for example, we would go to the beach with bread crumbs. We had a tradition of releasing the bread crumbs into the ocean, asking for forgiveness for those we had wronged. It was a beautiful tradition that brought our family closer together. These family gatherings strengthened our connection and brought more joy into our life.

Whether it's celebrating shabbat or sabbath or going to church on Sunday, these traditions offer a richness to our daily life. Traditions and rituals are integral to many religious and spiritual practices, offering numerous benefits that enhance joy and well-being. These activities provide structure and meaning to our lives, fostering a sense of continuity and connection to the past. Rituals, whether daily prayers, weekly services, or annual celebrations, create moments of reflection and gratitude, allowing us to pause and appreciate the present. They often involve community participation, strengthening social bonds and creating a supportive network. Additionally, traditions and rituals can serve as anchors during turbulent times, offering comfort and a sense of stability. By incorporating these practices into our lives, we can cultivate a deeper sense of purpose, belonging, and joy, enriching our spiritual journey.

MAKING SPIRITUALITY YOUR OWN

You don't need to adhere to a specific religion to experience the benefits of spirituality. You can cultivate your own spiritual practice that aligns with your personal beliefs and values. Here are some habits and actions you can take to bring spirituality into your life. For me, much of what I have shared in this book is how I bring spirituality into my life.

- Mindfulness and Meditation
- Journaling
- Nature Connection
- Acts of Kindness and Service / Giving
- Gratitude Practice
- Evening Reflection

It now seems funny as I write this. Everything I do is tied to my spiritual connection. It is very personal and will look different for each of us. Incorporating religion and spirituality into your life can greatly enhance your happiness and well-being. By adopting habits and practices that resonate with you, you can create a personalized spiritual journey that provides meaning, peace, and joy. Remember: Spirituality is a deeply personal experience. Explore different practices, find what works for you, and embrace the journey with an open heart and mind. Whether through meditation, acts of kindness, nature connection, or building a community, spirituality can be a powerful tool for creating a happier, more fulfilling life.

Spirituality and religion can add a profound dimension to your joy. These practices often emphasize the importance of appreciating the present moment, finding meaning in everyday experiences, and connecting with something greater than oneself. They encourage gratitude, compassion, and mindfulness, all of which are key to experiencing joy.

Religion and spirituality provide a sense of connection—to oneself, to others, and to a higher power or the universe. This connection can foster a deep sense of belonging and community. Engaging in communal activities, such as attending services, participating in group meditations, or joining a spiritual study group, can enhance your feelings of support and camaraderie.

Here are some habits you might want to add to your life.

- Read a Bible or religious text
- Go to church, temple, or place of worship
- Join a group (examples: Bible study group, meditation circle)
- Light a remembrance or prayer candle
- Pray
- And, of course, pretty much any of the habits listed in this book from mindfulness to meditation to acts of kindness.

	MON	TUE	WED	THU	FRI	SAT	SUN
Read the Bible or pray	X	X	X	X	X	X	X
Go to church or temple							X

CONCLUSION

THE JOY OF LIVING

"Enjoy the little things in life, for one day you'll look back and realize they were the big things."

– ROBERT BRAULT

LESSONS FROM YOUR FUTURE
I told you the story about being held up at gunpoint and how that changed my perspective on life. You don't have to have a near-death experience to achieve that perspective.

I have an exercise I want to take you through. If you were listening to this book, I would tell you to close your eyes. Since you're reading, follow along and then maybe sit with it and see what comes up.

I want you to imagine you are at the end of your life. You're on your deathbed.

How old are you? How do you look? How do you feel? Who are you surrounded by? When you look back at your life, what are you proud of? What impact did you have? Who will miss you? I want you to make this as real as you can. Truly picture it. Feel it. Make it powerful.

Do you have regrets? If so, what are they? Looking back, how were your relationships? How was your health? What are you proud of?

Sit with it. If you are feeling good, proud, accomplished, then good for you! If you are feeling remorseful, then guess what? You have a second chance.

What would you need to change now so that at the end of your life, you feel content?

Live as you want to be remembered. You are the designer of this life.

THE HAPPINESS SET POINT

Let's go back to the beginning of the book. Remember when we talked about happiness? I probably should have told you about a psychological theory that we all have a happiness set point. That's right. We are all genetically predisposed to a certain level of happiness. If you have a low set point, you probably struggle more with depression and sadness. Fifty percent of your set point is probably set by genetics. Ten percent is set by your life circumstances, and 40 percent is set by your activities. That's where your habits come into play. Your habits can have a big impact on your happiness. But let's get this clear: No one is happy all of the time.

THE HEDONIC TREADMILL

As humans, we tend to pursue one pleasure after the other and then fall back to our original set point of happiness. Think about the last thing you wanted to buy. You wanted to buy that shiny new car. You bought it, and soon you ended up as happy as you were before you bought the car.

We are bombarded with messages telling us if we buy this or buy that that we will be happy. There once was a time when you were wealthy if you had more than one pair of socks. How many pairs of socks do you have now? We have more material wealth than at any time in history, but it has not increased our levels of happiness. While I am not saying you have to live as a minimalist, it's a helpful reminder to pause before you make that next purchase.

JOIE DE VIVRE

This French phrase literally means "joy of living." Your *joie de vivre* is your delight in simply living your life. People who seem to enjoy life in a cheerful and spirited way are often described as having *joie de vivre*.

I am hoping as we come to an end that you have started to do some of the things that will help you find the joy of living. I'm hoping you realize that it's not as hard as we make it out to be. We are living in a unique time that is luring us into missing life. We are made to believe that the more we work, the better, and there is no limit to work, as we can now work in the nooks and crannies of the day. Social media and television are the temptresses that takes over our free time and make us believe that other people are living better lives than us. We make our happiness dependent on the outcome of something. We live thinking there is something to achieve or win on the other side of losing weight, making lots of money, achieving fame, buying a flashy car, fill in the blank) We just show up for the ride each day. The pursuit of happiness is tricking us into thinking that we need these things to be happy. And in that pursuit, we miss what life is. Life is made up of your daily experiences. It's made up of your relationships. Your struggles. It's what you do and what you pay attention to. Life is made up of the little things. To wrap your life up in joy, you must live on purpose.

Your life is precious. The days and hours pass, no matter how we choose to use them. So be intentional.

I cannot take away that life is hard. I cannot take away many things that will happen to you. But you can choose how you respond to hard things. We can choose how we live in our every day. What if every single day you did something that brings you joy? Why not? Who says you can't? You are the designer of your life. You decide. You are the one who says yes to what's in your life. I love the saying, "If it's not a hell yeah, it's a hell no." What if your life was made up of hell yeahs?

Go through this book and keep choosing habits or activities that will add more joy to your life. The idea is not to be perfect and not to do them all. Choose what lights you up. Try different things. And when you get off track—and you will—do not judge or beat yourself up. There is no benefit to that. Just acknowledge it, learn what didn't work, and come back.

I hope your life looks different a year from now. I hope you are getting into nature regularly. I hope you are having some adventures. I hope you are playing and finding gratitude in the day. Start paying attention to the little things that bring you joy. The warmth of a shower. The sound of birds outside your window. The taste of your coffee. The more you pay attention to the little things, the more you will enjoy your life. When you start to pay attention to these things, you will stop paying attention to what's missing. My wish for you is to spread joy throughout each day instead. It will look different for each and every one of you, because you are unique and special. You are creating a life, my friend. Live it. Share it. Love it. Enjoy the journey. And find the joy of living!

I shared at the beginning of this book how I felt like my life was in chaos before I started these strategies. I was a new mom, running a national business, and felt like I was always running on empty. I was very good at getting things done. Very good at goal-setting and achieving. But each day I felt drained. I was living for weekends and living for vacations. I felt like a hypocrite because people would come to me for answers on life balance. Yes, I was successful in work and motherhood, but, personally, something was missing. And I found that something was joy.

CONCLUSION

As we close this book, I hope you feel inspired and empowered to make changes that will bring more joy into your life. Embrace the wisdom of living intentionally and cherish the small moments that truly matter. Remember: You are the designer of your life. Each day you have the opportunity to create a tapestry of joy, love, and fulfillment.

Don't wait for weekends or vacations to find happiness. Infuse your everyday life with moments that make you smile and activities that light you up. When challenges arise, choose how you respond with grace and resilience. You have the power to shape your experiences and cultivate a life filled with purpose and joy.

Take the lessons and insights from this journey and apply them in ways that resonate with you. Try different things, discover what brings you joy, and be kind to yourself when you stumble. The goal is not perfection, but progress and intentional living.

Imagine the life you want and start building it today. Pay attention to the little things that bring you happiness, and soon you'll find that your life is rich with meaning and joy. Live fully, love deeply, and enjoy the journey. You have the power to create a beautiful, joyful life—embrace it with all your heart.

I hope you create a life you love to live.